Assemble
together

Sixty topical assemblies for secondary schools

Tony Castle

Kevin
Mayhew

This edition published in 1999 by
KEVIN MAYHEW LTD
Buxhall
Stowmarket
Suffolk IP14 3DJ

0 1 2 3 4 5 6 7 8 9

ISBN 1 84003 344 4
Catalogue No. 1500266

Cover design by Jonathan Stroulger
Typesetting by Richard Weaver
Printed in Great Britain

Dedicated to Thomas

without whose assistance
this book would never
have been completed.

Acknowledgements

The publishers wish to express their gratitude to the following for permission to include copyright material in this book:

Mrs P. E. Dale for the extracts by A. T. Dale from *New World* and *Winding Quest*.

Darton, Longman & Todd Ltd, 1 Spencer Court, 140-142 Wandsworth High Street, London, SW18 4JJ, for extracts from the *Jerusalem Bible*, published and copyright 1966, 1967 and 1968 by Darton, Longman & Todd Ltd and Doubleday & Co. Inc., and used by permission of the publishers.

Echo Newspapers, Newspaper House, Chester Hall Lane, Basildon, Essex, SS14 3BL, for the story about Richard Hughes' experience in the Fastnet Race in 1979.

Eugene Geissler for 'There Is A Season'.

Victor Gollancz Ltd, Wellington House, 125 Strand, London, WC2R 0BB, for the extract from *The Year of Grace* compiled by Victor Gollancz.

HarperCollins Publishers, 77-85 Fulham Palace Road, Hammersmith, London, W6 8JB, for the extract from *Precocious Autobiography* by Yevgeny Yevtushenko.

David Higham Associates Ltd, 5-8 Lower John Street, Golden Square, London, W1R 4HA, for 'How Many Heavens', by Edith Sitwell which is taken from *Collected Poems*, published by Sinclair Stevenson.

Palm Tree Press, Buxhall, Stowmarket, Suffolk, IP14 3DJ, for the story 'Climb the Dark Wall' by Nigel Sustins, which is taken from *The Young Christian's Annual*.

Mr and Mrs Pole for the poem 'My Answer' by Hilary J. Pole.

Laurence Pollinger Ltd, 18 Maddox Street, Mayfair, London, W1R 0EU, and the Estate of Frieda Lawrence Ravagli for the poem 'Phoenix' by D. H. Lawrence, which is taken from *The Complete Poems of D. H. Lawrence*.

The Rt. Revd. V. Sanmiguel for *Pastor in Kuwait*.

Solo Syndication Ltd, 49-53 Kensington High Street, London, W8 5ED, for the extracts from the *Daily Mail*.

SPCK, Holy Trinity Church, Marylebone Road, London, NW1 4DU, for extract from *All Desires Known* by Janet Morley.

Unless otherwise indicated, all Bible quotations are taken from the *New International Version*, © Copyright 1973, 1978, 1984 by International Bible Society. Used by permission of Hodder & Stoughton Ltd. All rights reserved. 'NIV' is a registered trademark of International Bible Society. UK trademark number 1448790.

The publisher has made every effort to trace the owners of copyright material and we hope that no copyright has been infringed. Pardon is sought and apology made if the contrary be the case, and a correction will be made in any reprint of this book.

Contents

OLD TESTAMENT THEMES

WORLD RELIGIOUS THEMES

FAMILY AND PEOPLE GROUPS

GENERAL THEMES

Introduction

The very first action of Christians, on the birth day of the Church, the day of Pentecost, was to assemble together. They have done it every week since.

Togetherness is one of the essential marks of Christianity. The description given in Acts 2:42-47 of the community of the first Christians leaves us in no doubt that there was no thought of being a Christian on your own. Christ calls his followers into a family relationship; we are to be his brothers and sisters, and brothers and sisters of one another. Christian teaching and practice run contrary to the individualism of our age.

While there are legal obligations to be fulfilled in providing school assemblies, wise headteachers know that good, well-prepared and regular assemblies in the daily life of a school reap incalculable benefits. They have a marked impact upon relationships within and without the school, and upon its ethos.

Most of the assemblies offered for use in this book are unashamedly Christian. The material assembled together here is structured in such a way as to be of use on a variety of occasions, in different ways and under varying conditions.

There are sixty assemblies arranged in seven sections, A-G. Each section has a different content slant:

- Section A (A1-A10) develops the theme of 'Community'. It is more open-ended than most of the others, offering the possibility of a link with PSHE and further development in the classroom.

- Section B (B11-B20) centres upon the Christian festivals of Christmas, Easter and Pentecost.

- Section C (C21-C25) uses an allegorical story to explore some of the basic themes of Christianity.

- Section D (D26-D35) uses Old Testament characters to explore themes of relationship with God.

- Section E (E36-E45) explores themes from the major world religions.

- Section F (F46-F53) takes the theme of 'Family and people groups'. This section could also be linked with the delivery of PSHE.

- Section G (G54-60) is composed of a selection of general themes of interest and value to young people.

It is my hope that, after using these assemblies for a short while, the user of this book will gain both the enthusiasm and the confidence to abandon these and then use the book as a resource for her or his own assemblies.

Tony Castle
Advent 1998

Scripture Readings

The Good News Bible is recommended for the Scripture readings.

Note on Suggested Hymns

The hymn numbers are quoted from the following publications:

HON   Hymns Old and New, New Century Edition

HONA   Hymns Old and New, New Anglican Edition

HONS   Hymns Old and New, with Supplement

OS   Our Songs

CHB   Children's Hymn Book

           all published by Kevin Mayhew.

COMMUNITY

A1 What is community?

INTRODUCTION
(not to be read out)

As the pupils gather for the assembly, a workman (a disguised member of staff) is seen to be on the stage (or in the area where the assembly is to take place) absorbed in a maintenance or repair job. When all are gathered, the assembly leader, having called for quiet, approaches the 'workman' who continues his work, oblivious to the presence of anyone else.

ROLE-PLAY

ASSEMBLY LEADER *(Aloud for all to hear.)* Excuse me, would you mind moving. Perhaps you could come back later and finish what you are doing?

WORKMAN Sorry, (Miss or Sir), I must get this finished now.

ASSEMBLY LEADER I'm afraid you'll have to go – we are just about to start assembly.

WORKMAN What's 'assembly'?

ASSEMBLY LEADER Well, it's when we all *(adapt as necessary)* get together as a community to think about things and gather our thoughts for the day.

WORKMAN What's a community?

At this point, four or five pupils, one at a time, walk on to the stage (assembly area) and say out loud, 'I'm me'. When the last has arrived, they join hands and say together, 'We're us'. They sit down where they are and immediately five more come, carrying posters or placards. The first has the word 'Family' on it; coming to the centre, the pupil carrying it says, 'A family is a community'. Next comes a card reading 'Neighbourhood' and the pupil says, 'The neighbourhood can be a community'. There follows 'Club' and 'Class' with 'A . . . is a community'. Last comes 'School'. When the pupil carrying this placard joins the others, standing in a line facing the assembled pupils, all together say, 'The school is a community'.

RECORD *(This is turned up as the placard-bearers sit down.)*
Grandma's party tonight, Paul Nicholas. RSO.
(Fade after a short time.)

COMMENT Why do we go to parties? To have a good time? To meet our friends? Just to be with a crowd? One thing is certain – you can't have a party just by yourself.

READING Len Steels, rugged and grey, gathered sobbing men and women into his arms and asked pathetically, 'What can a man say? What can a man do?' He couldn't cry. Not even when they told him he had lost ten members of his family, including four sons.

Scaffolding inside a cooling tower at a new power station in West Virginia, USA, unwound like apple peel, plunging them and 41 others to their deaths. Len, 54, who has battled against cancer for ten years, could hardly bear the grief shared by the little hamlet of Cow Creek, where all his family lived.

Local Police Sergeant Mike Comer said it all: 'This is a close community, where just about everybody is related. When one feels pain, we all feel pain.'

'Four boys – I lost four boys,' said Len. 'We was very close, me and my sons. I trust in God. He'll never put more on me than I can bear. He gets me through the rough spots. But Lord, it's hard.'

Only minutes before, he had stood, disbelieving, outside a makeshift morgue set up at the tiny fire station at Belmont, West Virginia. Yesterday he tried to draw comfort from his only surviving son, Robert, 35, who had been working nearby when the top of the cooling tower at Pleasant Power Station in the town of St Mary's suddenly collapsed.

COMMENT A community is a group of people that shares both good and bad times together.

PRAYER Almighty God.
We ask you to give your blessing to this school community.
Help all of us gathered here to work for greater togetherness and harmony.
May we care for one another and the health and well-being of every member
    of our community.
We ask this through Christ our Lord. Amen.

HYMN *Bind us together, Lord.* HON 58, HONS 62, HONA 60

A2 Need for one another

OPENING RECORD *He's your brother*, Abba. Abba's Greatest Hits. Epic.
(Fade after 1 minute 20 seconds.)

COMMENT The words 'treat him well, he is your brother, we depend on one another' come across very strongly. A few years ago there was a strike by lorry drivers. Now lorry drivers don't sound very important. We know that if, for example, doctors were to refuse to work the community would be very hard hit; but until the lorry drivers went on strike very few people even noticed them. The strike nearly ruined us all, so that for the first time we realised how much we all depend on lorry drivers to move all the things we need around the country. For example, no lorry drivers, no food in the shops! We depend on one another and working together makes life easier and happier for all of us.

READING A blind man and a lame man happened to come at the same time to a piece of very bad road. The blind man begged the lame man to guide him through his difficulties. 'How can I do that,' said the lame man, 'as I am scarcely able to drag myself along? But if you were to carry me I can warn you about anything in the way; my eyes will be your eyes and your feet mine.'

'With all my heart,' replied the blind man, 'let us serve one another.' So taking his lame companion on his back they travelled in this way with safety and pleasure. *Aesop's Fables*

ROLE-PLAY *A group of pupils (five to eight in number) wander onto the stage or assembly area, chatting quietly among themselves. They stand in a circle facing one another. A lone pupil enters, sees the group and quickly hurries away in another direction. A second pupil enters and walks confidently up to the group. He says 'Hello' and the group ignore him, closing up their ranks. He tries again and their indifference becomes hostile. He moves off. The group disperses and withdraws.*

RECORD *He's your brother*, Abba (or whatever was used at the opening).
(Volume turned up as the group disperses.)
Finish the track.

COMMENT *(Make a poster of the following, to display at this point.)*
'People are lonely because they build walls instead of bridges!' Some people make no effort to join in and become lonely; others try and are rejected. We must erect no walls to exclude others and be bridge builders instead.

PRAYER Break through, break through, Lord God.
Break through our meanness and narrow selfishness.
Make us care about our class-mates;
make us concerned about the lonely in our school;
make us realise the need we have for one another.
Open our eyes to our own selfishness,
that we may learn that we need others as they need us.
Give us patience,
give us reconciliation,
for your name's sake. Amen.

HYMN *A new commandment.* HON 1, HONS 39, HONA 4

A3 Communication

RECORD   Theme music from *Star Wars, Doctor Who* or *Star Trek. (Fade.)*

COMMENT   Communication between astronauts and ground-control is essential. Without it no space mission would be possible. Imagine what it would be like to be way out in space with no contact with earth.

   The same would be true if you were sailing, alone, around the world. A few years ago Naomi James, a young woman who sailed around the world on her own, had that experience. She tried to contact her husband Rob and failed.

READING   Some time after leaving the Canaries I began to lose track of time. Although I wrote the date each day in my ship's log, I wasn't aware of days in the usual sense; there was nothing to distinguish Thursday from Sunday, for example. I could expect no human contact (except via the radio) for the next two-and-a-half months when there would be a rendezvous off Cape Town.

   I passed the Cape Verde Islands on 4 October (Day 26) and the following day put through a call to Rob's father to find out if Rob had reached Cape Town. I learned that he was due to arrive next day.

   So on Day 28, I phoned Rob's father again. He told me that he had spoken to his son only five minutes previously and gave me a number to ring that evening. I was thrilled to think I would soon he talking to Rob. I made notes of the things I wanted to talk to Rob about and fiddled away until the time when he would be expecting the call.

   There had been delays on some previous calls. So, I put up the aerial and turned on the set some two hours before Rob was expecting me. I was ready to go, but when I picked up the handset to make the call – nothing happened. I stared at the radio for a minute, thinking there must have been something I'd forgotten to do, but no, everything seemed to be in order and still the radio remained dead.

   An hour later, I had a sick and desperate feeling. I'd done everything I could and had no idea what to do next; I couldn't believe it was a major fault, it just couldn't be, I kept telling myself. I'd found all the radio spares and changed some fuses, but to no avail. I washed the deck terminal with fresh water and even got out the instruction manual – I might as well have tried to learn Greek in one sitting. I even looked inside the radio, but that was so alarming I shut it again quickly.

   The thought of Rob waiting for my call that night, and perhaps for the next four weeks, made me feel quite desperate. I racked my brains to see if there was something I'd overlooked but there was nothing. I sat in utter dejection till I knew Rob would have given up waiting for my call. He would presume I'd not been able to get through and would wait again tomorrow . . .

   Slowly it dawned on me that I still had thousands of miles to go to Cape Town and unless I could hail a passing ship no one would know if I were alive or dead.

   For my part I never expected help to come from the radio, but I hated more than anything else not being able to relieve the anxiety of my family, who would be faced with total silence.

COMMENT   We've all seen and heard BT's humorous advertising on TV, 'It's good to talk'. How true that is! If there's good news we can share it; if there's a friend in trouble we can offer help. Being able to communicate is all-important.

But the power of speech also brings responsibilities. Listen to these words of wisdom from famous writers:

READER A Nature has given to man one tongue, but two ears, that we may hear from others as much as we speak. *Epictetus*

COMMENT That emphasises the importance of learning to listen well to others; it's a selfish person who 'hogs' all the conversation.

READER B There are few wild beasts more to be dreaded than a talking man having nothing to say. *Jonathan Swift*

COMMENT There's a saying that 'empty vessels make the most noise'. That can be true and 'gossip' often harms others.

READER C Gossip, unlike river water, flows both ways. *Michael Korda*

COMMENT If you tell tales about others, remember they too will certainly gossip about you when you are not there.

READER D Conversation is the image of the mind. As a man is, so is his talk. *Publilius Syrus*

COMMENT What we say and how we say it, shows others what we are really like inside. Let us close with these words of a simple poem.

READER A A wise old owl sat on an oak.
The more he saw the less he spoke;
the less he spoke the more he heard.
Why aren't we like that wise old bird?

PRAYER O God,
take control of me all through today.

Control my tongue,
 so that I may speak
 no angry word;
 no cruel word;
 no untrue word;
 no ugly word.

Control my thoughts,
 so that I may think
 no impure thoughts;
 no bitter, envious or jealous thoughts;
 no selfish thoughts.

Control my actions,
 so that all through today
 my work may be my best;
 I may never be too busy to lend a hand
 to those who need it;
 I may do nothing of which afterwards
 I would be ashamed.

All this I ask for Jesus' sake. Amen.

HYMN *Make me a channel of your peace.* HON 262, HONS 342, HONA 328

A4 Truth-telling

OPENING RECORD   Tchaikovsky's *1812 Overture*, op 49. Finale. *(Last minute and a half, fade.)*

COMMENT   The following reading describes a true event which took place in World War II, when the Russian armies were storming Berlin – the final moments of the war.

READING 1   'Get out, get out,' the old man cried. 'Get out, run for your lives. The SS have explosives in the cellar, get out.' The half-crazed caretaker's cries were totally ignored. No one believed him. Women and children poured into the once-smart departmental store to plunder what they could. In the distance the rumble of the Russian guns was getting ever nearer.

The caretaker abandoned his post at one of the doors – the hordes of plunderers had swarmed in the other doors and smashed the shop windows – and hobbled out to an old cycle. Without another look over his shoulder he cycled off as fast as he could.

Not two minutes after he had disappeared from view, while hundreds of desperate scavengers hunted for food and clothing, the floor of the store erupted in a tremendous earth-quaking explosion. No one in the building stood a chance. In a second or two floors went up and walls caved in. The explosives stored by the SS in the cellar had been detonated by a time bomb. Over 300 women and children died because they did not accept the truth of what the caretaker had told them. *Anon*

COMMENT   Truth is not always easy to listen to – especially when it doesn't seem to be to our advantage. Nor is it always easy to speak the truth. Think about these proverbs from around the world.

READER A   *From France:* 'Individuals may perish, but truth is eternal.'

(Pause between readings.)

READER B   *From India:* 'The name of God is truth.'

READER C   *From former Yugoslavia:* 'Tell the truth and run.'

READER D   *From Israel:* 'A half truth is a whole lie.'

COMMENT   We are social beings; we are beings that need others. We need good, happy relationships, but these cannot be built unless there is trust between people. Relationships can only be built if the truth is told.

READING 2   Real growth in art and life
comes to us from the outside
as well as from within,
comes to us from our relationships
with other things and other people.
It does not come to us
from within or from without,
but from within and without

at the same time,
so that we must always be building bridges.
Without bridges we go nowhere.
Eugene S Geissler. 'There Is A Season'

PRAYER O God,
you can see my inmost thoughts
and know me better than I know myself.
You understand the impulses I feel,
the ambitions I have,
the silent loneliness I experience.
Forgive me my sins against truth –
the untruth within me,
the half-truths, the evasions,
the exaggerations,
the trying silences that deceive,
the masks I wear before the world.
Help me to see myself as I really am,
fill me with the courage I shall need
if I am to seek the truth
and live in truth. Amen.

HYMN *Let all that is within me.* HON 230, HONS 301
I'm accepted. HONA 239, CHB 109

CLOSING RECORD Tchaikovsky's *1812 Overture,* op 49. Finale. *(Opening minute, fade.)*

A5 Personal responsibility

OPENING RECORD *Eye-level,* Simon Park. Columbia.

As record is played, eight pupils sit on the stage or assembly area, and after 30 seconds of the record, stand in a line facing the assembled gathering. The first, third, fifth and seventh remain standing while the others, spaced between them, bend their knees in a squatting position, then in time to the beat of the music and perfectly in unison (a practice will of course be necessary) with their companions they go up and down like a line of pistons. They stop when the music is faded out.

COMMENT We are not machines or puppets. We are human beings with free will. We do not move all the time like a line of pistons in a car engine or puppets on strings. What we do we are responsible for – whether it is good or bad.

READING 1 *Escape from the incredible hulk.*
It looked as if Doreen Smalley's last moment had come when the incredible hulk dropped in. 'I was playing patience when I heard this low rumbling noise,' she said yesterday. 'I looked out of the window and just couldn't believe my eyes. I saw what looked like a big tank coming towards the house. It hit the house with a tremendous bang.'

In fact it was a 12ft-high, 20-ton runaway mechanical digger which had been set on a backwards destructive path by a group of young vandals who by-passed 'stop' devices with two bent nails.

The digger started its trail of destruction a quarter of a mile away at a council compound in Bolton Road. It crossed three roads . . . demolished heavy iron fencing, trees and a lamp standard . . . then ploughed over an allotment before crashing to a halt against Mrs Smalley's home.

Damage is estimated at £50,000. Mrs Smalley's husband, Ron, who was on night shift at the time, reckoned yesterday that £45,000 of that damage was caused to the house. He said: 'It looks as if the house will have to be demolished.'

Mr Gordon Brown, the contractor who owns the digger, said: 'Somehow the vandals managed to by-pass the immobilisation system. It's fantastic how the machine managed to travel so far, but these things are just like tanks.'

Last night, West Yorkshire police said they were anxious to trace four boys seen running from the council compound. They are believed to be aged around 9 to 12. *Daily Mail*

COMMENT When the boys just mentioned were caught it would be untrue for them to say, 'It's not my fault' or 'You're always picking on me'. They deliberately did something which resulted in the destruction of a house. The owner of the digger said, 'Somehow the vandals managed to by-pass the immobilisation system'. To be mature and grown up we must learn to accept responsibility for what we do.

READING 2 Here is a maturity checklist. How do you rate?

A Maturity Check-up

1. A mature person does not take himself too seriously – his job, yes!

2. A mature person keeps himself alert in mind.

3. A mature person does not always view with alarm every adverse situation that arises.

4. A mature person is too big to be little.

5. A mature person has faith in himself which becomes stronger as it is fortified by his faith in God.

6. A mature person never feels too great to do the little things and never too proud to do the humble things.

7. A mature person never accepts either success or failure in themselves as permanent.

8. A mature person never accepts any one of his moods as permanent.

9. A mature person is one who is able to control his impulses.

10. A mature person is not afraid to make mistakes.

Leonard Wedel

PRAYER Give me, O Lord, a sense of responsibility.
Give me
    a sense of responsibility to myself,
    so that I may not waste the gifts you have given me;
    a sense of responsibility to my parents,
    so that I may repay them for all the love and care
      they have given me;
    a sense of responsibility to my school,
    so that all the patient teaching I have received
      may not be wasted;
    a sense of responsibility to my friends,
    so that I may not fail their trust in me.
Give me, O Lord, a sense of responsibility
    that I may grow to real maturity;
    this I ask through Christ your Son. Amen.

HYMN *Walk with me, O my Lord.* HON 441, HONS 582
Fight the good fight. HONS 140, HONA 128

RECORD Replay the opening record.

A6 Respect for self

OPENING RECORD   *Building my body,* Don Mclean. Prime Time. EMI.

ROLE-PLAY   Three members of staff are needed; if they can make any of the following statements (or similar ones) truthfully, so much the better. Standing where they can be clearly seen and heard, they make their comments.

STAFF 1   I'm slimming – with my new diet I lost nearly ten ounces last week.

STAFF 2   I go for a jog every morning – it makes me feel really fit.

STAFF 3   I gave up smoking last month – now I can really taste the flavour of food.

COMMENT   People diet to keep fit, run or jog to keep trim, give up smoking to take care of their health. It is very important to look after our bodies – we have only got one and we will never have another! Can you imagine life without being able to run and play games? Worse still, being unable to move a muscle and not even being able to see? Hilary Pole was such a person.

READING 1   Hilary started life just like any other child, healthy and strong. She grew up to be very good at games and dancing. She became a PE and dance teacher. Then quite suddenly a terrible disease struck. Hilary could feel and hear everything but she couldn't move. She couldn't move her hands or her feet, her arms or her legs. Eventually she couldn't move her mouth or her eyelids. She couldn't sing; she couldn't talk; she couldn't make a sound. Because she was unable to chew, or eat, she was fed through tubes and kept alive with a breathing machine.

The only thing Hilary could move was the big toe of her right foot. Her big toe would give a tiny flicker, $\frac{1}{16}$-inch, less than 2 mm, when she wanted it to. The only other thing Hilary could do was hear.

But Hilary didn't just give up and die. For ten years she carried on 'speaking' and smiling, praying and helping others – through her big toe. Yes, you heard correctly – she dedicated herself to helping other disabled people.

At first she had to spell the words out letter by letter, but after three years, science came to help Hilary and she got a Possum machine. This meant she was able to operate a whole range of switches – turn on the radio and, most important of all, operate a typewriter. Letters poured from her; she wrote poems and articles for magazines. She worked so hard for disabled people that the Queen wrote to tell her that she had been awarded the MBE medal for her brave work for others.

Sadly, two years later Hilary died while undergoing an operation to widen her airways. *Anon*

COMMENT   What a brave person! Hilary certainly had self-respect. Here is one of her poems.

READING 2   *My Answer*
I'm often asked if I am bored,
frustrated, lonely,
my life abhorred.
And so I answer,
'I am not' . . .

that now I can accept my lot,
remind the sadly shaking head,
'It is my body, not my mind, in bed'.

I'm rarely frightened or in pain,
for this
I thank my God again.
I have many loyal friends,
my joy in them despair transcends.
There's music, too,
books to read:
discontentment cannot breed.

Although I can no longer play,
I can listen
every day
to football, rugby, tennis, cricket,
imagination has no limit.
Add to this
a sense of humour
killing that 'depression' rumour.

Now I have my Possum too,
a miracle
in all men's view.
No longer do I have to wait,
my poems and letters to dictate;
just flick my toe
and type myself –
I have no time to brood on 'health'!
Hilary J. Pole

PRAYER   I asked God for strength that I might achieve;
I was made weak that I might learn humbly to obey.

I asked for help that I might do greater things;
I was given infirmity that I might do better things.

I asked for riches that I might be happy;
I was given poverty that I might be wise.

I asked for all things that I might enjoy life;
I was given life that I might enjoy all things.

I was given nothing that I asked for;
but everything that I had hoped for.

Despite myself, my prayers were answered;
I am among all people the most blessed.
Anon

HYMN   *Give me joy in my heart.* HON 135, HONS 159, HONA 153

CLOSING RECORD   Repeat part of opening record.

A7 Respect for others

OPENING RECORD   *Fantasy island*, MPeople. The Best of MPeople. BMG.

COMMENT   'We got the power.' Yes, we have the power to turn friends into enemies, or enemies into friends. It's easy to turn a brother or sister into an enemy by unkindness and disrespect. We must always try hard to avoid that. It is also possible to turn an enemy into a brother, by showing him or her respect.

READING 1   In 1941 Mama took me back to Moscow. There I saw our enemy for the first time. If my memory is right, nearly 20,000 German war prisoners were to be marched in a single column through the streets of Moscow.

The pavements swarmed with onlookers, cordoned off by soldiers and police. The crowd were mostly women, Russian women with hands roughened by hard work, lips untouched by lipstick and thin hunched shoulders which had borne half the burden of the war. Every one of them must have had a father or a husband, a brother or a son killed by the Germans.

They gazed with hatred in the direction from which the column was to appear. At last we saw it. The Generals marched at the head, massive chins stuck out, lips folded disdainfully, their whole demeanour meant to show superiority over their plebeian victors.

The women were clenching their fists. The soldiers and policemen had all they could do to hold them back.

All at once something happened to them. They saw German soldiers, thin, unshaven, wearing dirty, bloodstained bandages, hobbling on crutches or leaning on the shoulders of their comrades; the soldiers walked with their heads down.

The street became dead silent – the only sound was the shuffling of boots and the thumping of crutches.

Then I saw an elderly woman in broken-down boots push herself forward and touch a policeman's shoulder, saying: 'Let me through.' There must have been something about her that made him step aside.

She went up to the column, took from inside her coat something wrapped in a coloured handkerchief and unfolded it. It was a crust of black bread. She pushed it awkwardly into the pocket of a soldier, so exhausted that he was tottering on his feet. And now suddenly from every side women were running towards the soldiers, pushing into their hands bread, cigarettes, whatever they had.

The soldiers were no longer enemies. They were people.
Yevtushenko

COMMENT   Seeing others who we dislike as people like us, with a mum and dad, brothers and sisters and friends, is a start to trying to understand and respect them.

POSTER   A poster could be used at this point; one from a missionary society might be suitable.

READING 2   Here are practical suggestions from Benjamin Franklin on respect for others.

The best thing to give your enemy is forgiveness;
– to an opponent, tolerance;
– to a friend, your ear;
– to your child, good example;
– to a father, reverence;
– to your mother, conduct that will make her proud of you;
– to yourself, respect;
– to everyone, charity.

HYMN   *Whatsoever you do.* HON 452
Help us to help each other, Lord. HONA 208

CLOSING RECORD   *All you need is love,* Beatles. Parlophone.

A8 Judging others

OPENING RECORD *Noye's Fludde*, Benjamin Britten. 2NF1 track: 'Mrs Noah's refusal'. (Introduce by describing what *Noye's Fludde* is.)

COMMENT Could you make out the words of Mrs Noah's attitude?
That's what we call 'prejudice'. But what is prejudice?

READING 1 Jimmy Savile calls it 'abuse of the mind'. He says how he dislikes abuse of the mind, and tells of one of his frequent trips to Northern Ireland when he met a nice lady and said to her, 'How do you get on with the violence?' She said, 'It's awful, Jimmy, but the danger is that we're learning to live with it now. We've come to expect it and we just look at it and read about it and learn to live with it. It is a great sadness to us.' Then she carried on in the same tone of voice, 'I will never be happy until every Catholic in Northern Ireland is dead.' It saddened Jimmy beyond measure, because the dear lady was abusing her mind. He felt it was an abuse of the mind to want to kill either Protestants or Catholics, or anybody or anything.

COMMENT Let us listen to what a few famous writers have to say about 'abuse of the mind' or prejudice.

READER A 'Prejudice is the child of ignorance.' *William Hazlitt*

READER B 'To be prejudiced is always to be weak.' *Samuel Johnson*

READER C 'Prejudices are what rule the vulgar crowd.' *Voltaire*

READER D 'The man who never alters his opinion is like standing water, and breeds reptiles of the mind.' *William Blake*

COMMENT It is possible to change your opinion; to think deeply and rid your mind of any abuse that may fill it.

READING 2 Air Commodore MacDonald Somerville saw a young punk rock group tramp out into a hazardous Scottish blizzard and succeed in rescuing a couple who almost certainly would otherwise have died.
'I always thought of pop groups as hairy kids pumping away on their ukuleles,' he says, 'but these are very fine young fellows with a terrific social conscience.
'We've all got trenchant views, blinkered prejudices, and the tendency to slap labels on people. This might teach some of us to accept that punk rockers can be brave . . . teenagers can be responsible . . . missionaries can be bounders.'
Daily Mail

COMMENT The air commodore came to realise that he had been quite wrong about a certain group of young people; but he was prepared to learn and change his opinion. We must all aim to have open and informed minds, free from abuse.

PRAYER   Almighty God,
help us not to abuse our minds;
help us not to judge others by appearances.
Help us, Lord, to understand
that no matter what colour we are
or what age, or what we believe,
we are all equally your sons and daughters.
May we never intentionally
give hurt or offence to anyone;
help us to realise that,
if we are all your sons and daughters,
that makes us brothers and sisters in your family.
We ask for your help through Christ our Lord. Amen.

HYMN   *Let there be love shared among us.* HON 232, HONS 726, HONA 298

CLOSING RECORD   Repeat opening track from *Noye's Fludde.*

A9 Personal integrity

ROLE-PLAY These are four very short role-plays. The four can take place in the same assembly or area, pupils standing up to perform their piece and then sitting down again where they are.

ROLE-PLAY 1 *A pupil is obviously waiting for someone – strolls up and down, looks at watch. Another pupil appears and goes to walk by. First pupil says,* 'Where have you been, I've been waiting half an hour.'

'Sorry,' *says the second,* 'I changed my mind. I'm going with Paul instead.' *He then walks on unconcerned.*

COMMENT Integrity means you can be relied upon.

ROLE-PLAY 2 *Two pupils wander into view. The first says,* 'You can trust me. I'll not tell anyone, honest.'

'Well, all right,' *says the second. They whisper together for a moment. The second says,* 'See you later', *and disappears. Another pupil appears and the first goes deliberately up to him – they whisper then start laughing.*

COMMENT Integrity means you can be trusted.

ROLE-PLAY 3 *Child-adult role-play; one pupil should be taller and apparently older than the other.*

'Dan,' *says the adult,* 'I've told you before, don't do that.'

'But, Dad,' *says Dan,* 'you do it all the time.'

'That's got nothing to do with it,' *says Dad.* 'It doesn't matter what I do, you do what you are told.'

COMMENT Integrity means there's a unity and no inconsistency between what you say and what you do.

ROLE-PLAY 4 *Child-adult role-play (as above).*

'I'm all ready, Dad, what time are we off?'

Dad replies, 'We're not going.'

'Why not?' *asks his son.*

'Well, I forgot all about it, and now I'm too busy,' *replies the father.*

'But you promised,' *says the son.* 'You've promised before and we didn't go.'

COMMENT Integrity means you are a person of your word.

READING This story shows that integrity can sometimes demand bravery, to match words with deeds.

During World War II, the people of Giazza (pronounced 'Jatza'), a village north of Verona, decided not to co-operate with a unit of German paratroopers stationed in their village. The commanding officer retaliated. He arrested a group of villagers and threatened to shoot them. The parish priest, Father Domenico Mercante, pleaded for his people and offered himself in their place. The Germans accepted his offer and prepared to execute him. One of the firing squad refused to shoot the priest. For his disobedience he was placed next to the priest and both died together. The soldier's name is not known.

Years passed and on the sixteenth anniversary of their deaths, on the spot where they died, a white monument to the two heroes was erected. Present at the ceremony was the Bishop of Verona, the German ambassador to Italy and the Italian Minister of Justice who said, 'The example of a priest and soldier dying by the same rifle-fire, in order that not only the written law but the unwritten law too should be respected, provides an example of great moral value. It gives rise to the hope that the cause of peace amongst men may find its strongest protection in the conscience of humble but heroic spirits.'

COMMENT 'In the conscience of humble but heroic spirits.' That means ordinary people like you and me being brave about standing up for real values.

PRAYER O Lord and Master
You know us better than we know ourselves.
Like an X-ray, your Holy Spirit can see through us
and search out our weaknesses and our fears.
Pour your love into our hearts
that we may become
the sort of people you want us to be. Amen.

HYMN *I, the Lord of sea and sky.* HON 186, HONS 712, HONA 235

A10 Respect for property

OPENING RECORD *Money, money, money,* Abba. Epic.

COMMENT Do you remember *Oliver*, the musical based on Dickens' book *Oliver Twist?* In *Oliver* Fagin had a school for pickpockets who went out to make money by picking the pockets of the rich. Gangs of pickpockets still 'work' in London today. Nowadays, they concentrate on the crowds of ordinary people and tourists in groups and on the London Underground.

ROLE-PLAY *Pupil wheels an imaginary bike (a real bike would be better!) into view, stands it up against a wall and goes into a shop. Another pupil comes along, looks around and gets on the bike. He's just about to ride off when the first pupil appears and says,* 'Oi, what are you up to, that's my bike!'
'Sorry,' *says the second pupil,* 'I was only borrowing it for a ride.'

COMMENT Taking something which is not ours, without permission, is stealing (or shoplifting); 'borrowing' a classmate's biro and not returning it, could be stealing. There's a character in *Oliver* called, you'll remember, the Artful Dodger. If you are an artful dodger you could be a thief.
To dodge paying your fare on the bus deliberately is to steal. You have taken a ride for nothing. Our attitude should be that we want to share and give rather than take.

READING Jimmy Savile describes how he tries to use such monies as he has to do the sort of work of which he thinks God might be proud – sorting out a few human beings. But he warns that you have to be very, very careful about giving money away; you can actually ruin people. You have to be very sensitive about what you do with money, in principle. He isn't bothered by having large sums of money around him because he's forever doing things with the money, and he doesn't exploit anyone to get it.

COMMENT Jimmy Savile is saying, 'It's not what we have that's important, but the sort of people we are.'

PRAYER Lord God,
help me to respect myself.
I have only one life
which I can only live once.
Life is precious.
I am precious in your sight.
Help me to remember
that each person is unique and special.
Help me, too, to respect your creation
and the things of nature.
Help me to respect other people's property,
for you have told us that whatever we do to others
we do to you. Amen.

HYMN *I give my hands to do your work.* HON 184, HONS 235
One more step along the world I go. HONA 405, CHB 166

CHRISTIAN FESTIVALS

B11 Christmas 1 – Emmanuel

OPENING RECORD   Handel's *Messiah:* Chorus, 'For unto us a child is born'.

COMMENT   That stirring opening chorus is from the *Messiah* by George Frederick Handel. Just before that piece of music, there are the words, 'The people who walked in darkness have seen a great light'. Handel himself knew what it was to be depressed and to experience darkness.

READING   One night in 1741 a bent old man shuffled listlessly down a dark London street. George Frederick Handel was starting out on one of his aimless despondent wanderings. His mind was a battlefield between hope and despair. For 40 years he had written stately music for the kings and queens of England, but now the court society had turned against him. Four years before he had suffered a cerebral haemorrhage, which had paralysed his right side, making it impossible for him to walk and write. But now, aged 60, with England in the grip of a hard winter, he felt old and helplessly tired.

As he walked he passed a church, and welling up from within him came the cry, 'My God, my God, why have you forsaken me?' He returned to his shabby lodgings. On his desk was a bulky package. He opened it and his eye fell on the words, 'He was despised and rejected of men'. Reaching for his pen he started to write. Notes filled page after page. He worked almost non-stop for 24 days, taking little rest and even less food. When the *Messiah* lay finished on his desk he collapsed on his bed and slept for 17 hours. This tremendous masterpiece, one of the greatest ever composed, is now a traditional part of both Christmas and Easter.

COMMENT   Handel was not the first to imagine he was abandoned by God, only to find that God was with him all the time.

READER A   God asked Moses to go to the Egyptian Pharaoh and get his people released from slavery, but Moses was afraid. He said to God, 'Who am I to go to Pharaoh and bring the sons of Israel out of Egypt?'

'I shall be with you,' God answered. *Exodus 3:12*

COMMENT   God chose Joshua to take Moses' place as the leader of the Israelites, but he too was afraid.

READER B   God said to Joshua, 'As long as you live, no one shall be able to stand in your way; I will be with you as I was with Moses; I will not leave you or desert you.' *Joshua 1:4*

COMMENT   God asked Gideon to lead 300 men against an army of thousands from Midian. Gideon was terrified.

READER C   'I can't do this,' said Gideon. 'My clan is the weakest and I am the least important person in my family.' God answered him, 'I will be with you and you shall crush the tribe of Midian as though it were a single man.' *Judges 6:15*

COMMENT   What happens when God sends his Son to be the Light of the World?

READER D   'The Lord himself, therefore, will give you a sign. It is this: The maiden is with child and will soon give birth to a son whom she will call Emmanuel.' *Isaiah 7:14-15*

COMMENT   Emmanuel means 'God is with us'. God was with Handel and he achieved a great and wonderful work. God was with Moses, with Joshua and Gideon; they had no need to fear, all they needed was faith. We have that faith and believe that we have no need ever to fear, for God came and lived among us. And that is why Christmas is so special.

RECORD   (Turned up to fade in on the above comment) *Messiah:* Chorus, 'For unto us a child is born'. *(Fade out for the prayer after 30 seconds to one minute.)*

PRAYER   Almighty Father,
you sent your Son Jesus to be the Light of the World,
the God-with-us.
When all seems dark and depressing
help us to trust in your loving presence
and remember that you are always with us
whether we are enjoying good times or bad.

HYMN   *The Virgin Mary had a baby boy.* HON 411, HONS 550, HONA 496

B12 Christmas 2 – Christ's birthday

COMMENT Did you know that the very first Christmas card was sent in 1844, by a Mr Dobson? The first cards to be sold publicly in the shops didn't arrive for another two years, in 1846. The first company to produce large numbers of cards for sale was Tucks – who still make and sell cards – in the year 1870. It's hard to imagine Christmas now without cards, rather like birthdays without birthday cards.

Is it anyone's birthday today? Or tomorrow? Let's now sing *Happy Birthday to you*

SONG *Happy Birthday to you.*

COMMENT Why don't we sing 'Happy Birthday' on Christmas Day, for Jesus, instead of singing carols? It is his birthday, after all.

READING 1 The first Christmas that little Linda learned to read she was allowed to distribute the family gifts from under the tree on Christmas morning. According to family custom the one who distributed the gifts could open the first package. After all the presents were distributed with loving care, Linda kept looking and looking around the tree and among its branches. Finally her father asked, 'What are you looking for, dear?' to which Linda replied, 'I thought Christmas was Jesus' birthday and I was just wondering where his present is. I guess everyone forgot him!' *Anon*

COMMENT I wouldn't be surprised if many of you could *not* tell me when your parents' birthdays are. Those of you who could tell me the date, I'm sure would not know the time of day your mother or father was born. If the day is so important, why don't we know more about it?

Another thought for you. Have you noticed that we usually only keep the birthdays of living people? So it's not the *day* that matters but the person.

READING 2 Birthdays are not about *days* but about *persons*.

When my Dad's birthday comes round and I give him a card and a present, I'm not really interested in what day of the year it is, I'm interested in him. My present says, 'I love you and I'm glad you're around.' I'm celebrating and being thankful for my father's continuing existence and all he's done for me. *Anon*

COMMENT So at Christmas we are saying thank you to Jesus for still being with us. On his birthday we celebrate that he is alive and among us still.

PRAYER On Christ's birthday, Almighty Father,
we think too much of ourselves.
Our thoughts centre upon presents, cards, parties and food;
we give little thought to your Son and his birthday.
Help us, this Christmas, not to be so selfish.
May we remember what we are celebrating.
May we be grateful that your Son is alive and among us
this Christmas and always. Amen.

HYMN *From heav'n you came, helpless babe.* HON 130, HONA 148, CHB 52

B13 Christmas 3 –
The dignity of the individual

OPENING RECORD *Mary's boy child*, Boney M. Atlantic. *(Fade.)*

PLAY/READING There follows an anonymous poem that can be used as a play, play-reading or reading.

MARY Now praise the Lord that led us
so safe into the town,
where men will feed and bed us,
and I can lay me down.

JOSEPH And how then shall we praise him!
Alas my soul is sore
that we no gifts can raise him.
We are so very poor.

MARY We have as much as any
that of the earth do live;
although we have no penny,
we have ourselves to give.

JOSEPH Look yonder, wife, look yonder!
A hostelry I see,
where travellers that wander
will very welcome be.

MARY The house is tall and stately,
the door stands open thus;
yet, husband, I fear greatly
that inn is not for us.

JOSEPH God save you, gentle master!
Your littlest room indeed
with plainest walls of plaster
tonight will serve our need.

HOST For lordlings and for ladies
I've lodging and to spare;
for you and yonder maid is
no closet anywhere.

JOSEPH Take heart, take heart, sweet Mary,
another inn I spy,
whose host will not be chary
to let us easy lie.

MARY O aid me, I am ailing,
my strength is nearly gone.
I feel my limbs are failing;
and yet we must go on.

JOSEPH	God save you, hostess. Kindly, I pray you, house my wife, who bears beside me blindly the burden of her life.
HOSTESS	My guests are rich men's daughters and sons, I'd have you know! Seek out the poorer quarters where ragged people go.
JOSEPH	Good sir, my wife's in labour, some corner, let us keep.
HOST	Not I; knock up my neighbour and as for me, I'll sleep.
JOSEPH	Good woman, I implore you, afford my wife a bed.
HOSTESS	Nay, nay, I've nothing for you, except the cattle shed.
MARY	Then gladly in the manger our bodies we will house, since men tonight are stranger than asses are and cows.
JOSEPH	Take heart, take heart, sweet Mary, the cattle are our friends. Lie down, lie down, sweet Mary, for here our journey ends.
MARY	Now praise the Lord that found me this shelter in the town, where I with friends around me may lay my burden down.

COMMENT Have you ever noticed that Jesus started life in someone else's cattle shed and died 30 years later and was buried in someone else's grave. Mary and Joseph had to 'seek out the poorer quarters where ragged people go'. They were poor, but at that moment, they were the most important people in the world. It's not what you have and own in life that matters – it's what sort of person you are. What matters is your dignity as an individual.

Litany prayer

READER When I say 'Lord, in your birth', please answer, 'We find our worth'.

In Bethlehem, on the first Christmas Day, people put the rich before the poor. May we learn that all people are equal, for
Lord, in your birth
we find our worth.

In Christ's life there were few possessions. May we learn to put acquiring virtues before acquiring things, for
Lord, in your birth
we find our worth.

In the quiet of the stable the Prince of Peace was born, and in the fields the angels sang 'Goodwill to all men'. May we be people of inner peace seeking to spread the peace of Christ, for
Lord, in your birth
we find our worth.

In our celebration of Christmas we so easily forget that our dignity as persons springs from the Word of God becoming one of us. Help us, Lord, to realise our dignity and worth, for
Lord, in your birth
we find our worth.

HYMN   *See, amid the winter's snow.* HON 358, HONS 471, HONA 439

B14 Easter 1 – Christ's sacrifice and death

OPENING RECORD   Handel's *Messiah*, part two: Chorus, 'All we like sheep have gone astray'. *(Fade after 1 minute 40 seconds.)*

COMMENT   That magnificent chorus from Handel's *Messiah* reminds us that the whole human race had strayed away from God, rather like sheep wandering off without a shepherd to care for them. Christ came as our Good Shepherd to lead us back to God.

(For acting out the following story two pieces of wood are required, one longer than the other, joined together in the shape of a cross with a screw or nail, so that the cross-piece is movable. Four pupils are required to wander on stage, pick up the wood in turn, and use it as directed.)

READING   Once upon a time there were two pieces of wood, fastened together by a nail, and they lay on the sands, where every day, when it was time, children used to come and play.

Twice every day the tide came in and carried these pieces of wood backwards and forwards, leaving them on a different part of the beach each time. But when the tide had gone out the two pieces of wood were always there waiting for the children when they came onto the sands.

Lee came down early one morning, picked up the two pieces of wood which were very wet because the tide had only just gone out and he began to rush around the beach playing at aeroplanes. *(Pupil uses the cross as an aeroplane.)* But after about ten minutes he became tired and when he saw one of his friends coming down, he threw the two pieces of wood down and ran to meet him.

The next person to find the wood was a little boy of 7, called Peter. He came down to the sands after his tea and watching his favourite TV programme about pirates. So when he saw the pieces of wood he picked them up and began prancing around as though he were a pirate attacking a Spanish galleon. *(Pupil brandishes the cross as a sword.)* But the sea was creeping in, and over on the road Peter could see his father looking for him, so he left the wood to be carried to and fro once more by the tide.

The next day was a Saturday, and that afternoon the beach was crowded with people who had come for a day out. Among these were Mr and Mrs Simpson and their son Paul, aged 10, and it was not long before Paul stumbled over something and picked it up.

'Look, I've got a machine gun,' he shouted. 'A-a-a-a-a-a-a-a-a.' *(Pupil holds cross-bar vertical, putting it up to his eye and using it as a gun.)*

After tea, Susan came down to the sands with her dog, Sandy. She liked to come down as often as she could to throw pieces of old driftwood into the sea, because Sandy liked nothing better than to run into the water and carry them back to Susan. She looked this way and that along the beach for a suitable piece of wood, and at last her eyes rested on the wood which Paul had been playing with a short time before. 'This will do,' she thought. She went across, pulled it out of the sand and straightened the cross-piece – and held it up like this †. *(Pupil holds cross up as described.)* 'Wow, it's a cross!' she said, 'like the one Jesus died on. I wonder why no one has seen it before. It's a shame to leave it here. I'll take it to church and we can use it next week in our Easter Garden. It'll look great there.' *Anon*

COMMENT There is a beautiful Anglo-Saxon poem, probably written about the year AD 750, over 1,200 years ago, which views Christ's death for us on Calvary from the point of view of the cross itself. In other words, you have to imagine it is the cross speaking. Here are some extracts from the poem.

READER A Listen to me
I want to tell you the best dream I ever had.
It happened in the middle of the night
When all men everywhere were sleeping in their beds.
It was just as if I saw a wonderful tree
towering up into the sky.
It seemed to be filled with light,
brighter than any light you've ever seen:
the whole gleaming shape was covered with gold.
And then I heard it begin to make a sound:
the wood itself, the best wood that could be found,
began to talk to me like this:

READER B It was a long time ago . . .
but I can still remember it.
I was at the edge of the forest:
the last tree in the row.
They cut me down:
left my roots behind.

Strong enemies there took me away:
they told me to hold their criminal up high:
they made me into an exhibition.

Men carried me on their shoulders,
set me up on a hill.
And there a crowd of enemies
fastened me firm in the ground.

Then I saw the Lord of all mankind
hurry towards me eagerly,
he was determined to climb up on me.

He was intent on saving humankind
the world over,
and I trembled as he
laid himself upon me
in a kind of embrace.

But I still dared not bend down to the earth,
or fall to the ground.
I had to stand up straight.
I was a cross.
I held up high
the King himself: the Lord of Power.

34

The Lord of Heaven above:
how could I stoop down?

They pierced me with dark nails:
you can still see the scars quite clearly:
open wounds, inflicted by men of hate,
but I was powerless to harm them.

The crowd mocked us both:
I felt the moisture of the blood
from the man's side,
and then he let his spirit flee,
and died.

There were many grim experiences for me
on that hill.
Donald G. Butler (ed.), 'Many Lights'

POSTER   Poster of Crucifixion from *The Footsteps of Christ* by Benedictine Nuns of Turvey Abbey. Available from McCrimmons.

SONG/HYMN   *Were you there when they crucified my Lord?* HON 449, HONA 540, sung by a soloist, group or the whole assembly; or repeat the opening record track.

B15 Easter 2 – Risen Lord

OPENING COMMENT An important part of our business in this school is to impart and acquire knowledge. But there are different kinds of knowledge, or we can 'know' in different ways. For example:

READER A I know French, I speak with a good French accent.

READER B I know my way through London, I've often been there by car.

READER C I know how to surf the Internet; I also use e-mail instead of letters.

READER D I know the Chairman of the FA; I can get Cup Final tickets.

READER E I know Christ is alive and living with us.

RECORD Handel's *Messiah*, part three: Air, 'I know that my Redeemer liveth'. *(Fade after 2 minutes.)*

COMMENT Thomas the Apostle came to know that Jesus was alive. He would not believe when he was told by the other friends of Jesus. He had to learn the truth of it for himself.

DRAMATIC READING Cast: narrator, Jesus, Thomas, and a small group.
Scene: the upper room in Jerusalem.

NARRATOR The first day of the week passed and it was now late in the evening. The friends of Jesus were together in the house. They had locked the doors because they were frightened of the Jewish leaders. Then – there was Jesus, standing among them.

JESUS Peace be with you.

NARRATOR With these words, he let them see his hands and his side. They saw it was Jesus and were utterly amazed.

JESUS Peace be with you. The Father sent me on a mission; now I'm sending you.

NARRATOR There and then, he gave them God's power.

JESUS Receive the gift of the Holy Spirit

NARRATOR That evening one of the friends of Jesus was absent – Thomas, who had the nickname, 'the twin'. When he returned there was a surprise for him.

GROUP (Speaking together) We've seen the Lord. We've seen Jesus.

NARRATOR Thomas was amazed when they told him this. His friend was dead, how could they have seen him!

THOMAS I don't believe you. I won't believe until I've seen for myself. I must see and touch his wounds before I believe!

NARRATOR The following Sunday, all the friends of Jesus were together. Thomas was with them this time. The room was locked because they feared arrest and the same fate as Jesus. Suddenly there he was among them.

JESUS Peace be with you.

NARRATOR Then he turned to Thomas.

JESUS Here are my wounds. Where are your fingers? See, touch. Touch my hands, and my side too! You must show that you trust, that you believe in me.

THOMAS My Lord and my God. I do believe.

JESUS Do you believe in me and trust me just because you have seen me with your own eyes? Happy are the people who will trust me without ever having seen me with their own eyes.
Alan Dale, 'New World'. Based on John 20:19-29.

PRAYER
READER Happy are we if we can say, 'I know my redeemer lives'. Please join in this response: Lord, we know you are alive and to be found among us.

I am risen and can be found among you.
Lord, we know you are alive and can be found among us.

I am risen and you can hear my words in the words of the Bible.
Lord, we know you are alive and can be found among us.

I am risen and can be found in service to your neighbour.
Lord, we know you are alive and can be found among us.

I am risen and among you when you are gathered together in my name.
Lord, we know you are alive and can be found among us.

I am risen and you can find me in the breaking of bread.
Lord, we know you are alive and can be found among us.

CLOSING RECORD Handel's *Messiah*, part two: 'Hallelujah chorus'.
(Fade in 'King of Kings . . .')

or

CLOSING HYMN *Come, Lord Jesus, come.* HON 95, HONS 104
Alleluia, alleluia, give thanks to the risen Lord. HON 26, HONS 14, HONA 24

B16 Easter 3 – Living Lord

OPENING SONG/ HYMN *Morning has broken* (HON 269, HONS 350, HONA 337) may be sung, or play the record: Cat Stevens. Island.

COMMENT On the very first morning of creation, the world was probably a fiery ball of gas. With the resurrection from the dead of Jesus, the Son of God, we have a new creation: 'Morning has broken like the first morning.'

ROLE PLAY *Four pupils enter, one carrying a large Easter candle (the local parish church might be kind enough to lend theirs for the occasion). The candle has been prepared with long white paper streamers, about an inch wide, attached to the top of the candle. The candle is held aloft and the other pupils, taking hold of the streamers, walk slowly round the candle. The streamers wind round the candle, maypole fashion. Meanwhile a comment is made.*

COMMENT On the streamers are your names, written (yesterday/this morning or whenever) in your own handwriting. At your christening you were given a candle as a symbol of your oneness with Christ, the Light of the World. The streamers have become one with the candle – you are one with Christ the Light of the World. *(The candle is placed in a central position.)*

READING 1 One ancient symbol of Christian belief in the resurrection is the phoenix. This bird symbolised hope and the continuity of life after death.

According to legend, only one phoenix could live at a time. The Greek poet Hesiod, writing in the eighth century BC, said it lived nine times the lifespan of the long-living raven. When the bird felt death approaching, it built itself a pyre of wild cinnamon and died in the flames. But from the ashes there then arose a new phoenix, which tenderly encased its parent's remains in an egg of myrrh and flew with them to the Egyptian city of Heliopolis, where it laid them on the altar of the sun god. These ashes were said to have the power of bringing a dead man back to life.

Scholars now think that the germ of the legend came from the Far East, and was adopted by the sun-worshipping priests of Heliopolis as an allegory of the sun's daily setting and rebirth.

In Christian art the resurrected phoenix became a popular symbol of Christ risen from the grave.

COMMENT The phoenix is an ancient symbol of the resurrection of Christ. The writer D. H. Lawrence has a poem that applies the symbol to our lives.

READING 2 *Phoenix*
Are you willing to be sponged out, erased, cancelled,
made nothing?
Are you willing to be made nothing?
Dipped into oblivion?

If not, you will never really change.

The phoenix renews her youth
only when she is burnt, burnt alive, burnt down
to hot and flocculent ash.
Then the small stirring of a new small bub in the
nest with strands of down like floating ash,
shows that she is renewing her youth like the eagle,
immortal bird.
D. H. Lawrence

COMMENT Our baptism candle was given to us with the words, 'Keep this flame burning brightly'. We can only do that if we try to stay close to Christ, the Light of the World.

PRAYER Christ has no body on earth but yours;
no hands but yours;
no feet but yours.
Yours are the eyes through which is to look out
Christ's compassion to the world.
Yours are the feet
with which he is to go about doing good.
Yours are the hands
with which he is to bless people now.

HYMN *Now the green blade riseth.* HON 285, HONS 376, HONA 355

B17 Pentecost 1 – Symbol of fire

COMMENT   If I were to shout out now, 'Fire, Fire,' and the fire alarm sounded, you would probably think, 'It's not a fire drill this time, or a false alarm, but the real thing'. Some of you might be frightened. Fire can be frightening – think of the fear of people trapped by fire in a hotel or big store, or in the film *Towering Inferno*.

READER A   Fire can destroy – I often help my dad burn the dried weeds and leaves in the garden.

READER B   Fire can be welcoming – we have a coal fire at home and when I come in wet and cold from football in the winter, it's great to sit by the fire.

READER C   Fire is strong – I went on an outing once to an iron foundry where we saw great cauldrons of melted iron, taken out of the massive furnaces. It was awesome.

READER D   Fire can give light – I remember when there was an electricity strike and we only had candles alight in the house. I was surprised how much light one candle gives.

COMMENT   Fire has been important to man over the centuries – for cooking as well as light; for warmth and life too. Listen to this extract from a story by Jack London, about a man travelling in the Arctic in weather seventy-five degrees below freezing point. He is travelling alone in snow-covered country and has just fallen and got his feet wet.

READER A   He would have to build a fire and dry out his footgear. This was imperative at that low temperature – he knew that much; and he turned aside to the bank, which he climbed. On top, tangled in the underbush about the trunks of several small spruce trees, was a highwater deposit of dry firewood – sticks, and twigs, principally, but also larger portions of seasoned branches and fine, dry last year's grasses. He threw down several large pieces on top of the snow. This served for a foundation and prevented the young flame from drowning itself in the snow it otherwise would melt. The flame he got by touching a match to a small shred of birch bark that he took from his pocket. This burned even more readily than paper. Placing it on the foundation, he fed the young flame with wisps of dry grass and with the tiniest dry twigs.

   He worked slowly and carefully, keenly aware of his danger. Gradually, as the flame grew stronger, he increased the size of the twigs with which he fed it. He squatted in the snow pulling the twigs out from their entanglement in the brush and feeding them directly to the flame. He knew there must be no failure. When it is seventy-five below zero, a man must not fail in his attempt to build a fire – that is, if his feet are wet.

   But he was safe. Toes and nose and cheeks would be only touched by the frost, for the fire was beginning to burn with strength. He was feeding it with twigs the size of his finger. In another minute he would be able to feed it with branches the size of his wrist, and then he could remove his wet footgear and, while it dried, he could keep his naked feet warm by the fire, rubbing them at first, of course, with snow. The fire was a success. He was safe.

COMMENT   But he wasn't; a moment later a branch-load of snow cascaded on the fire and buried it. After he had recovered from his bitter disappointment he desperately swung his arms to and fro to try to get warm, then tried again. But his fingers were now frost-bitten and he had to light the bark holding the matches in the palm of his hand.

READER B   At last, when he could endure no more, he jerked his hands apart. The blazing matches fell sizzling into the snow, but the birch bark was alight. He began laying dry grasses and the tiniest twigs on the flame. He could not pick and choose, for he had to lift the fuel between the heels of his hands. Small pieces of rotten wood and green moss clung to the twigs, and he bit them off as well as he could with his teeth. He cherished the flame carefully and awkwardly. It meant life, and it must not perish. The withdrawal of blood from the surface of his body now made him begin to shiver and he grew more awkward. A large piece of green moss fell squarely on the little fire. He tried to poke it out with his fingers, but his shivering frame made him poke too far, and he disrupted the nucleus of the little fire, the burning grasses and tiny twigs separating and scattering. He tried to poke them together again, but in spite of the tenseness of the effort, his shivering got away with him, and the twigs were hopelessly scattered. Each twig gushed a puff of smoke and went out.

COMMENT   That was his last living effort – shortly afterwards he died of the bitter cold. As Jack London's story was read, did you feel your hope rising with the freezing man? Then crash as his hopes died! The fire meant life; no fire, no life!

Throughout the Bible the Spirit of God has been symbolised as fire. That which gives life – which warms – which lights up life.

SCRIPTURE READING   Acts 2:1-3.

PRAYER   Come, Holy Spirit, give life to our souls, light up our minds with your fire; destroy our selfishness and warm our hearts with the fire of your love. Make us clean within, by your purifying fire, so that we may better serve the Son of God and give greater glory to the Father. Amen.

HYMN   *Holy Spirit, Lord of Light.* HON 179, HONS 216
Spirit of the Living God. HON 377, HONS 501, HONA 454

B18 Pentecost 2 – Symbol of wind

COMMENT Newspaper headlines like MIRACLE, followed by the story of how Essex yachtsman, Tony Bullimore, in 1996 survived the mountainous waves and gale-force winds of the Southern Ocean amazed us.

Here is the story behind another headline: 'How I survived the waves of death.' In 1979 the famous Fastnet yacht race, from Cowes on the Isle of Wight to Ireland and back – round the Fastnet Rock – ran into the most terrible storm ever experienced in that area. Many boats were lost, 138 people were rescued, and 17 yachtsmen lost their lives. This is one man's story in a local evening paper.

READING A Southend yachtsman has spoken of the most terrifying experience of his life – the storm-hit Fastnet Race. Richard Hughes, 29, of Westcliff, relived the nightmare of the disastrous race that claimed the lives of 17 sailors. He was one of the nine-man crew on the 37-foot yacht, *Zap* – a sister ship to the Burnham boat, *Trophy*, which lost three men.

Richard is an experienced yachtsman but it was his first Fastnet Race. He has sailed in a transatlantic race and endured a hurricane in the Bermuda Cup ocean race. He said: 'I have sailed through a hurricane, but it was nothing like this. This storm was so severe for so long. The waves were mountainous – the height of a double-decker bus. Great high walls were topped with rolling crests that smashed against the boat. At first we had too much sail up. We were racing so fast the speedo was off the clock.'

Richard said luck and applied seamanship saved his yacht from catastrophe. Safety harnesses stopped him being washed overboard as he struggled along the deck. As he looked back, a wave engulfed the yacht and he saw his helmsman up to his chest in water. 'It was terrifying. The waves were smashing over us and the boat was gyrating about at all angles. Crew morale was low. We were about two-thirds of the way to Ireland when the storm struck,' said Richard.

Zap wandered up and down the Irish coast for a day and night before getting into Cork harbour.
Basildon Evening Echo

COMMENT Mountainous seas in a storm are caused by the wind, which whips up the waves. The wind is a very powerful force.

READER A It can drive windmills. The wind can be harnessed for good, to pump water and grind grain.

READER B It can dry washing on the clothes line and be a cooling breeze on a very hot day.

READER C The wind can be gentle – and fun when I fly my kite!

READER D The wind is an invisible power which blows where it will!

COMMENT The wind is a perfect symbol for the Holy Spirit. The Spirit of God is also an invisible force that moves where it wills – and with power.

SCRIPTURE READING Acts 2:1-4.

READING *(These are the words of a song which may be sung if the melody is known.)*
Where does the wind come from?
Where is it going?
You see the swaying tree,
and all the grasses blowing.
You know the wind is there,
but where?
There is no knowing.

Where does the Spirit come?
Where is his dwelling?
You see the weary world
so wilful, so rebelling.
But still the Spirit breathes
and where
there is no telling.
Sister Mary Oswin

PRAYER Come, Holy Spirit, breath of God,
blow away the cobwebs of selfishness within us
and guide us to a close union with Jesus,
to the glory of God the Father. Amen.

HYMN *Come from the north.* HON 89, HONS 97
O Breath of Life. HONA 356

B19 Pentecost 3 – Symbol of breath

COMMENT Have you ever seen a truck with a crane-like attachment pick up a big waste bin in the streets? A great heavy weight – lifted by air!

Without air your football or your bike tyres aren't much use. A football lacks form – 'life' if you like – without air; your bike becomes 'dead', useless, if there is no air in the tyres.

Have you ever watched *999 Lifesavers* on the TV? Here is a role-play inspired by that programme.

ROLE-PLAY *The scene is a busy beach in the middle of the summer holidays. A group of teenagers sees a boy in trouble out in the sea (group drifts on to the stage or area, talking together).*

One of the group cries out, 'Look, someone's drowning, come on, Tony'. *Two boys disappear. Others stand looking anxiously, then one comments,* 'They've got him – here they come'. *Another says,* 'Come on, let's help'. *A boy is hauled into view, unconscious. One of the rescuers says,* 'What shall we do now?' 'I'll go for an ambulance' *says one girl.* 'I'll call the police,' *says another.* 'No, no,' *says a third,* 'That will all be too late. He needs the kiss of life. I've learnt it at Scouts. Quick, out of the way.' *He kneels down by the boy, puts him in the recovery position and gives the kiss of life. Unconscious boy slowly recovers. Sits up. Girl who rushed off to get ambulance comes back, calling* 'The ambulance is here'.

COMMENT It must be a wonderful experience to bring someone back to life; we should all know how to do that. God first breathed life into us.

SCRIPTURE READING Genesis 2:5-7.

COMMENT The Holy Spirit breathes new life into Christians so that they may live more fully for God and those around them.

READING *Wind of God*
Holy Spirit,
mighty wind of God,
inhabit our darkness,
brood over our abyss,
and speak to our chaos;
that we may breathe with your life,
and share your creation,
in the power of Jesus Christ.
Amen.
Janet Morley, 'All Desires Known'

HYMN *Breathe on me, breath of God.* HON 67, HONS 70, HONA 69

B20 The Holy Trinity

COMMENT The most terrible punishment that can be inflicted upon a person is to be cut off from every other human for a long period; it is called solitary confinement. It is such a terrible experience because we are each made to love and be loved – we are made to be with others.

READER A In the 1980s an ITN reporter interviewed a missionary working in Malaysia with the 'Boat People' – the thousands of refugees driven out of Vietnam and escaping in old battered boats. Only half of the tens of thousands ever arrived in a new country; the rest were lost at sea in storms, or drowned when boats sank, or attacked and killed by pirates. The ITV newsman said to the missionary, 'Does the depressing sight of these poor people make you doubt the existence of God?'

'No,' replied the missionary, 'it convinces me that there must be something better than man. There must be a power of love beyond man.'

READER B St Augustine was a great Christian thinker and writer who lived about AD 400. One day he was walking along the sea-shore thinking about the mystery of the Trinity and how he could best describe it in a book he was writing. Close by he saw a little boy, who had dug a hole in the sand and was running to and fro to the sea with his bucket, pouring water into the hole. 'What are you trying to do?' asked Augustine. 'I am going to put all the sea into that hole,' replied the little boy. Yes, thought Augustine to himself, that is like me, trying to put into human words the vast mystery of God.

He went home and wrote his book about the Trinity, in which he says that God is love, therefore, there must be somehow more than one in God; that the Father and Son love each other and the Love which proceeds from them is the Holy Spirit. That is the nearest we can get to so deep a mystery.

PRAYER
READER To every third invocation, please reply, 'Praise and glory to your name'.

Father, creator of our vast universe,
Father, creator of our daily world,
Father, giver of life and love,
Praise and glory to your name.

Son of God, saviour of all,
Son of God, sharer of our daily world,
Son of God, giver of life and love,
Praise and glory to your name.

Holy Spirit, inspirer of truth and love,
Holy Spirit, comforter in our daily world,
Holy Spirit, giver of life and love,
Praise and glory to your name.

HYMN *Holy, holy, holy, Lord God almighty.* HON 177, HONS 215, HONA 212

CHRISTIAN CALLING AND LIFE

C21 Christian vocation

OPENING RECORD (*Background*) Stravinsky's *The Rite of Spring*. Track: 'The sacrifice'. ASD. (*Fade.*)

COMMENT Today we start a serial – a story told in five parts over the next five assemblies. The story is by Nigel Sustins and is called *Climb the Dark Wall*.

The writer takes us to a land of the future where everyone is ordered around by the Government's guards; there is no freedom and everyone has to work for the Government in factories.

READING They sat cross-legged on the ground in a circle. Tim was the one with the sandy hair and wandering eyes, Maureen with the swinging black pony-tail, Douglas pale and thin-faced, Jenny with cheeks the colour of sun-ripened apples and Philip was the tallest of them. They were trying to hold down a fit of the giggles as the teacher droned on, turning over oily pieces of machinery that were meant to fit into a sensible shape.

Machines! That was all they were ever taught about. 'Tomorrow,' said the teacher, without taking his dull unblinking eyes off the metal pieces, 'you will visit the factory where you will work as soon as you are old enough.'

'What excitement,' they thought!

The next day a ramshackle old truck groaned into their commune and they crouched down in the back, ready to discover the delights that lay ahead in their adult life when they would be able to work for the state. At midday the truck rattled to a halt and the 'teachers' (they were really black-uniformed state guards) made the children get out and sit at the roadside to eat a quick lunch. A cloud seemed to pass over the sun as they chewed their rations and the guards started to nod off into sleep.

'That's odd!' said Tim. 'These fellows must work harder than we thought!' There was a crunch of boots on the roadway and the children looked up to see the remarkable face of a stranger. He was bearded and sun-tanned, with travel-stained outdoor clothes, a rucksack on his back and a coil of rope over one shoulder. His eyes gleamed good-humouredly.

'They sleep soundly, the mindless ones! Come! We'll have a different lesson today. I've something more interesting than factories to show you.'

'But . . . who are you?' asked Philip. 'Where have you come from?'

'The hills. I'm a mountaineer. Call me Eagle. I sometimes climb as high as that bird even without wings.'

He was walking away from them, and they all looked at each other, shrugged their shoulders and followed.

COMMENT The important word in that story, which sums it all up, is 'Come'. The stranger calls Tim, Maureen, Douglas, Jenny and Philip to follow him.

SCRIPTURE READING Matthew 4:18-22.

COMMENT Jesus called quite a number of people to follow him, to be his disciples, but not all answered the call.

SCRIPTURE READING Matthew 19:16-22.

PRAYER Almighty Father,
your Son calls us to follow him,
to live the Christian life.
It is not easy to live up to what he asks of us,
so please give us the strength we need
to answer his call courageously and generously. Amen.

HYMN *Follow me, follow me.* HON 122, HONS 145, CHB 50
Father, hear the prayer we offer. HONA 120
or replay opening record.

C22 Baptism

OPENING RECORD   Stravinsky's *The Rite of Spring*. Track: 'Dance of young maidens'. ASD. *(Fade.)*

COMMENT   Today we continue our futuristic serial *Climb the Dark Wall*. Last time you will remember, Tim, Maureen, Douglas, Philip and Jenny were called away from a boring monotonous life by Eagle, the strange traveller.

READING   Eagle stopped at the edge of a swift stream. 'First lesson,' he said, uncoiling his rope and linking them all together with a loop round each waist. 'Let the rope be your lifeline. Feel it between your fingers and trust it.'

Eagle plunged straight into the stream.

'Hey!' shouted Maureen. 'Hang on! I've had a bath this week already!'

'Don't be timid. Come on. Trust the rope.'

One after another they waded into the rapid current until they were up to their chins in water. They could just see Eagle climbing up the bank on the other side in front of them. They had to go right under, mouths shut tight, and feel the pull of the rope drawing them through the stream. They all dripped on the grass together, looking very sorry for themselves.

'Don't worry,' said Eagle. 'We'll dry out. Second lesson: a little rock-climbing.'

They'd never had such a stiff climb in all their lives before, but Eagle shouted out instructions – where to place hands and feet and how to balance the body – and they managed to haul themselves to the summit of a grey-stone crag that overhung the valley.

'There!' said Eagle, pointing downwards. 'Smoke, factory walls. Chimneys like sooty fingers poking at the sky. They call it progress! Why do they love their walls so much?'

'S'pose they want to keep all the people in,' said Jenny. 'Otherwise, we'd all be off: no stopping in those rat-holes.'

'They also want to hide something,' said Eagle. 'Look: we can catch a glimpse of it from up here.' He pointed into the distance where the puffy clouds over the mountain-tops thinned, and the children saw brief gleams like sunshine on smooth lakes or glinting from green-gold forests.

'Beautiful!' said Douglas. 'Where is it?'

'My land. I want to take you there. But first you have to learn to climb. Because before we can get to my land, we have to scale the daddy of all black walls. It's built like a battleship and twice as thick.'

COMMENT   'Trust the rope,' said Eagle, as they all plunged one at a time through the water. We became Christians when we were baptised. Then we started a new life of faith and trust in God – that's the rope in the story which held them together, safe, as one united group.

PRAYER
READER   After each sentence please answer, 'No one can enter the Kingdom of God unless they are born through water and the Spirit.' This needs to be either written large on card for all to see, or use an OHP.

Jesus said, 'Lay not up for yourselves treasure upon earth, but lay up for yourselves treasure in heaven.'

No one can enter the Kingdom of God unless they are born through water and the Spirit.

Jesus said, 'Unless you become like little children you shall not enter the Kingdom of God.'
No one can enter the Kingdom of God unless they are born through water and the Spirit.

Jesus said, 'What you do for the least person you do for me.'
No one can enter the Kingdom of God unless they are born through water and the Spirit.

Jesus said, 'Love your enemies, do good to those who dislike you.'
No one can enter the Kingdom of God unless they are born through water and the Spirit.

Jesus said, 'Ask and you shall receive, seek and you shall find, knock and the door will be opened to you.'
No one can enter the Kingdom of God unless they are born through water and the Spirit.

POSTER   While the above is being said, a suitable poster, picture or photograph can be displayed if available.

HYMN   *The Lord's my shepherd.* HON 405, HONS 534, HONA 490
or replay the opening record.

C23 Eucharist

OPENING RECORD *(Background)* Stravinsky's *The Rite of Spring.* Track: 'Mystical circle of the young maidens'. ASD. *(Fade.)*

COMMENT We continue now our serial story, *Climb the Dark Wall.* Maureen, Tim, Douglas, Philip and Jenny have gone with Eagle away from the dark city to live in the mountains.

READING It was a wonderful time – living in the hills with Eagle, and feeding on the coarse brown bread he produced and the refreshing drink that glowed in their veins like wine. But – too soon as far as they were concerned – he spoke to them one day with tight lips and a grim face.

'We've got to go down. Face the black wall. There's no escaping it.'

They picked their way through gullies and over rockfalls and came down to a darkened valley where the weak light that managed to struggle through showed up the grains of dust and grit littering the air. The wall reared its head like a black, square-faced whale on the peak of a tidal wave. Blank. Forbidding. Definitely saying: 'No through way.'

'How do we get over that?' whispered Maureen.

'Courage. Skill. And trust in your rope.' said Eagle. 'Now I'm going to . . .' He stopped in mid-sentence and cocked his ear to listen. 'A jeep!' he hissed. 'Patrol! Quick – up that bank and into the bushes, and keep the rope in your hands.'

'What are you going to do?' asked Philip.

'Climb the dark wall. It's beaten men for too long.'

'But the danger . . .'

'The danger is to be content with that ugly monster blocking out our joys and hopes. Someone has to climb the wall, or the fear of it will drag us all down to death.'

COMMENT As part of their training with Eagle the children ate 'the coarse brown bread'. In our journey through life we may receive the bread to eat which is the Body of Christ. Bread which gives us the strength to go on.

PRAYER

READER After each sentence please answer: 'Lord, you are with us; may we find strength in the breaking of bread.' (Words could be displayed on a clearly visible card or OHP.)

Jesus said, 'Do not work for food that cannot last, but work for food that endures to eternal life.'
Lord, you are with us; may we find strength in the breaking of bread.

Jesus said, 'My Father gives you bread from heaven, the true bread which gives life to the world.'
Lord, you are with us; may we find strength in the breaking of bread.

Jesus said, 'I am the bread of life. He who comes to me will never be hungry.'
Lord, you are with us; may we find strength in the breaking of bread.

Jesus said, 'If you do not eat the flesh of the Son of Man and drink his blood, you will not have life in you.'
Lord, you are with us; may we find strength in the breaking of bread.

Jesus said, 'He who eats my flesh and drinks my blood lives in me and I live in him.'
Lord, you are with us; may we find strength in the breaking of bread.

HYMN   *Feed us now.* HON 119, HONS 138
I am the bread of life. HON 183, HONS 226, HONA 222
Alternatively replay the opening music.

C24 Faith

OPENING RECORD   Stravinsky's *The Rite of Spring*. Track: 'Sacrificial dance'. ASD. *(Fade.)*

COMMENT   We left our story *Climb the Dark Wall* with the group led by Eagle at the foot of the dark wall. They hear a jeep coming . . .

READING   The children hurried away into the bushes, and Eagle approached the wall. He rubbed his hands over the rough pitted surface and stared hard at it as if he could move it by force of will. The sound of the patrol jeep grew louder. With painful slowness Eagle gripped the wall with fingers and toes and started to inch his way up the vertical climb. He breathed heavily but clung to the surface as if he were glued to it.

The jeep screeched to a standstill. A black figure rose up from the back seat and extended the silver nozzle of a high-velocity rifle. An ear-splitting whine, and Eagle was knocked off the wall as if he had been a fly.

Black-booted guards gathered round his body, kicked him and laughed. They dragged him towards the wall, and levered up a slab of stone which covered a gaping hole: a kind of tomb, airless and cold. Eagle's body was dumped inside the hole, and then the stone rammed home again. Sealed. Utter blackness.

The jeep grated its gears and drove off. The children looked out from the bushes with white sweating faces.

'Why?' asked Jenny, crying. 'What do we do now?'

'We wait,' said Tim. 'As he said, we've still got the rope.'

And all through the rest of that day and into the night that followed, they clung to the rope, feeling it to be indeed their only lifeline.

COMMENT   'We've still got the rope,' said Tim. They still had faith and hope, although all seemed desperate.

SCRIPTURE READING   Luke 23:44-49.

PRAYER
READER   Let us pray for the lonely, the depressed and the bereaved.
To each invocation please reply, 'Lord, help us to believe in you and trust you.'

For those who are dying and are afraid; give them strength and courage:
Lord, help us to believe in you and trust you.

For those who have been wounded by the death of someone they love:
Lord, help us to believe in you and trust you.

For those who are very ill and are in pain:
Lord, help us to believe in you and trust you.

For those who live in the darkness of loneliness and depression:
Lord, help us to believe in you and trust you.

When we are lonely, frightened and fed up:
Lord, help us to believe in you and trust you.

When our parents, teachers and friends seem to misunderstand us and we feel like running away from it all:
Lord, help us to believe in you and trust you.

When we find it hard to believe in your love and care:
Lord, help us to believe in you and trust you.

HYMN *Give me joy in my heart.* HON 135, HONS 159, HONA 153
Look around you. HON 241, HONS 316
or replay the opening record.

C25 Mission

OPENING RECORD Stravinsky's *The Rite of Spring*. Track: 'Dance of the adoration of the earth'. ASD. *(Fade.)*

COMMENT Our story *Climb the Dark Wall* finishes today. Last time Maureen, Tim and the others were left alone after the death of Eagle.

READING It was still dark. But they sensed a change in the air. A humming. Enemy aircraft? No. A throbbing, like a huge sob or cheer about to break out. Then they heard the roar of an explosion. They tumbled head over heels out of the bushes and down the slope towards the black wall. Slowly they got to their feet. The rope: it was pulling, pulsing with life, tugging them up against the wall. They felt all over the black surface, and it seemed to them as if they were looking downward into the black ice of an enormous frozen lake. Then their hands broke through the ice and they were wriggling their fingertips in air: an open space. A pin-prick of light sprang up as from a great distance, and started to spin round like a catherine wheel, gaining in size and speed as it spun down a black tunnel towards them. Suddenly: bright flame. Like the sun. Of course: the sun rising beyond the wall. They were seeing through the wall. No sooner had they realised that when a figure rose up in the tunnel – a human shape rimmed with fire. Eagle stepped out in front of them, the early sunlight flicking in his hair.

'Eagle!' they cried, breathless with wonder and excitement.

'What a climb!' he said, smiling at them. 'I have fallen to great depths, but see – I have climbed back again. The fear of death has left me unmarked.'

'But how? . . . We saw you shot . . . walled up . . .'

'Enough!' he said, raising his hand. 'This wall will never be impassable again. I have opened a way that can never be closed.'

'And can we go through?' asked Douglas. 'Into your land?'

'Not yet. You all have a job to do first of all. Bring more people to this place. Draw them from all parts of the world, from every nation and race. You have my rope and my promise of help. Join all humankind – yes, all the universe – into the bonds of my rope which bring freedom.'

They stood looking at him, amazed, tired, joyful, bewildered. He laughed and went from one to the other ruffling their hair.

'Go on, children. Go with my blessing.'

And they looked at each other, shrugged their shoulders and went.

COMMENT 'Go with my blessing', Eagle said. The group were sent out.

SCRIPTURE READING Matthew 28:16-20.

COMMENT If we really believe that Christ rose from the dead then we have an obligation to work and pray for more people to believe that too.

PRAYER

READER Please respond to each invocation with the words, 'May your kingdom come.'

Christ, our leader and friend,
we pray that all may come to know and love you.
May your kingdom come.

That all people may work together to make the world a happier, more peaceful place to live in.
May your kingdom come.

That the world's food and energy may be shared for the greatest good of all.
May your kingdom come.

That the delicate balance of nature may not be destroyed by human greed or bad judgement.
May your kingdom come.

That all the world's children may have the opportunities of education and good health.
May your kingdom come.

That all people may learn to give dignity and respect to each and every one of their neighbours, whatever their race or religion.
May your kingdom come.

Let us now say the prayer that Jesus taught us:
Our Father . . .

HYMN *Colours of day.* HON 79, HONS 87, HONA 87
God's Spirit is in my heart. HON 152, HONS 183, HONA 180
or replay the opening record.

OLD TESTAMENT THEMES

D26 Trust in God

OPENING RECORD *Bright eyes,* Art Garfunkel. CBS. *(Introduction 1 minute 20 seconds.)*

COMMENT Once upon a time there was a wealthy Edomite sheik called Job, the most outstanding sheik in all the East. He was, moreover, a good man, a genuinely innocent man. His religion was real religion and he would have nothing to do with evil of any kind. He had a large family – seven sons and three daughters – and immense wealth.

READING

NARRATOR One day God summoned the Heavenly Court. It met in his presence and among the members of the Court was the Satan, God's Inspector General. God turned to him.

GOD Where have you been?

SATAN On the earth. I've been wandering north, south, east and west.

GOD Did you come across my servant Job? Now there's a good man for you – a genuine and innocent man. His religion is real religion and he won't have anything to do with evil of any kind.

SATAN Yes, I met him. He's a good man, I admit. But then he has every reason to be! He has nothing to fear – you stand guard over him and his family, and his immense wealth. Indeed, it is you who have made him as wealthy as he is. But just touch that wealth of his – or his family – and he'll curse you to your face!

GOD Very well, he's in your hands – you do just that. But leave the man himself alone.

NARRATOR Then Satan left the Court. *(Pause.)* One day the people were having a banquet at Job's eldest son's house. Job himself was not there, he was at home when disaster struck. One after another, messengers came running with bad news.

FIRST MESSENGER — Arab raiders have carried off the oxen and asses from the fields and murdered your herdsmen! I'm the only one to escape!

SECOND MESSENGER — Lightning has killed all your sheep and the shepherds! I'm the only one to escape!

THIRD MESSENGER — Wild tribes from the desert – three bands of them – have driven off all your camels and killed all your camel-drivers! I'm the only one to escape!

FOURTH MESSENGER — A desert hurricane has blown your son's house down! The young people at the party were buried in the rubble – and they're all dead! I'm the only one to escape!

NARRATOR — Job was hard hit. But he knelt down in prayer:

JOB — I came naked from the earth,
to the earth I shall go naked back.
God gave,
God takes back:
blessed be his name!

NARRATOR — All through these disasters Job never lost his trust in God, or said a word against him.
Then things got even worse for Job. God allowed Satan to tempt him further.
Satan went back to earth. He struck Job with boils from head to foot, and Job sat itching in the ash-pit, scratching himself with a piece of broken crockery.
His wife scolded him.

JOB'S WIFE — And you still trust God! Curse him – and die!

JOB — That's a wicked thing to say. You're just talking street gossip! You know that we must take God on his own terms, whether it's good or evil that he sends. That's no more than our duty.

NARRATOR — Job is left with nothing – not even good health; but Satan does not shake his trust in God.

Play the record 'Bright eyes' (as above); fade to background for reading.

God gave Job everything back – indeed he made him twice as wealthy as he had been before.

His fellow tribesmen and friends held a banquet in his honour. They sat down together at table and consoled him for all the misfortunes he had gone through. They each gave him a silver coin and a gold ring.

Job's wealth was now immense. And he had a second family – seven sons and three daughters, as before. The girls were the most beautiful girls in the world (he called the youngest 'Bright Eyes') and in his will he went beyond the law and treated them like their brothers.

He lived for a long time after this. He had great-great-grandchildren, and was a very old man when he died.
Alan Dale, 'Winding Quest'

PRAYER   *Psalm 139*

Lord, you examine me and know me,
you know if I am standing or sitting,
you read my thoughts from far away,
whether I walk or lie down, you are watching,
you know every detail of my conduct.

God examine me and know my heart,
probe me and know my thought;
make sure I do not follow evil ways,
and guide me in the way that is everlasting.

HYMN   *Yahweh, I know you are near.* HON 462, HONS 620
Lord of all hopefulness. HON 250, HONS 329, HONA 313

59

D27 Reconciliation

OPENING RECORD   *We don't talk anymore,* Cliff Richard. EMI. *(Fade after 1 minute 30 seconds.)*

COMMENT   'We're not speaking to one another', you hear people say when they've fallen out with someone. God never 'falls out' with us – it's we who fall out with him. Like King Ahab who approves of a terrible crime by his wife.

READING

NARRATOR   Naboth was a farmer. His vineyard had belonged to his family for hundreds of years and lay next to the palace grounds in Jezreel City. One day King Ahab asked Naboth about it.

KING AHAB   I'm wanting a vegetable garden. Your vineyard is just what I want – it's just next door to my palace. Will you let me have it? I'll give you a better vineyard for it; or I'll pay you a fair price, just as you like.

NABOTH   No, that vineyard was my father's and my grandfather's. I should be an irreligious man if I sold my ancestral lands.

NARRATOR   The king went back to his palace a vexed and sullen man; he'd set his heart on that vineyard. He went to bed and sulked and wouldn't have anything to eat.

QUEEN   Why are you sulking?

NARRATOR   He told what had happened. She was a foreign princess and was thinking of what her father, the King of Tyre, would have done.

QUEEN   You're a fine king. Get up and eat your food and stop worrying. I'll see you get the vineyard.

NARRATOR   She sent a royal letter, sealed with the royal seal, to the aldermen and freemen of the city, all Naboth's fellow-councillors.

QUEEN   Proclaim a religious fast, and put Naboth where everybody can see him. Get two witnesses – you know what kind of men to get – to sit facing him and to charge him with cursing God and the king. You know what the sentence is – death by stoning.

NARRATOR   The city council carried out the royal orders to the letter. They held the fast, suborned the witnesses and had Naboth executed outside the city. They sent a brief report: 'Naboth has been executed.'

QUEEN   Get up and go down to the vineyard. It's yours now. Naboth wouldn't sell it to you, would he? Well, he's dead!

NARRATOR   The king got up and went down to the vineyard to take possession of it. (By law the property of rebels and criminals became the king's.) God spoke to Elijah:

GOD   Get up and go and meet King Ahab face to face. He's in Naboth's vineyard; he's gone to take possession of it. Give him this message from me: 'You've committed murder to get hold of a vineyard. Where the street dogs are licking up Naboth's blood, they'll one day lick up yours!'

KING   *(to Elijah)* Have you caught up with me, my enemy?

ELIJAH   I've caught up with you all right. You've sold your soul in this foul deed; you've signed your own death-warrant – and that of your family. 'I'll get rid of you all!' says God.

NARRATOR   When King Ahab heard these words, he tore his robes and wore sackcloth. He accepted Elijah's rebuke.

COMMENT   King Ahab is shattered when he realises the evil his wife has led him into. He cries out to God in sorrow.

PRAYER   *Psalm 130*
From the depths I call to you, Lord.
Lord, listen to my cry for help!
Listen compassionately
to my pleading!

If you never overlooked our sins, Lord,
Lord, who could survive?
But you do forgive us:
and for that we revere you.

COMMENT   Our song which follows reminds us that we too have failed in our relationship with God – we too need God's forgiveness.

HYMN   *God forgave my sin.* HON 145, HONS 175, HONA 167
Oh, the love of my Lord. HON 323, HONS 430, HONA 398

D28 God on our side

COMMENT
In modern times the Israeli army has proved itself to be one of the best in the world. In Old Testament times the Israelites won many battles with God helping them. This one, during the revolt King Saul led against the Philistines, was won through the bravery of Jonathan, the king's son.

READING

NARRATOR Saul's troops numbered 600. He and Jonathan set up camp at Gibeah. The Philistines held Michmash and sent out three raiding parties to capture strategic points in the highlands and the main body of the Philistines at Michmash pushed out an outpost to the heights of the Michmash Pass.
One day Jonathan spoke to his young armour-bearer:

JONATHAN Let's go and have a look at the Philistine outpost over there on the other side of the Pass.

NARRATOR Saul had taken his stand, with his 600 soldiers, outside Gibeah, where he had his headquarters under the pomegranate tree by the threshing-floor. Jonathan said nothing about his plans to his father; even the soldiers didn't know he'd gone off.
Now on either side of the Michmash Pass there were two steep cliffs, one on each side, north and south. (Their local names were 'Slippery Rock' and 'Thorny Rock'.)

JONATHAN Let's go over to those heathen Philistines. God will be on our side – he doesn't depend on numbers.

ARMOUR-BEARER Go ahead. I'm your man!

JONATHAN Now listen. We'll let them see us. If they shout at us, 'You stay where you are till we get at you!' we'll just stay put. But if they shout, 'Come on up and try your luck!' then up we go. That's a sure sign God's put them at our mercy.

NARRATOR They both stepped out and let themselves be seen.

PHILISTINE SENTRY Look, the highlanders are coming out of their hide-outs!

NARRATOR The sentries hailed the two men.

SENTRIES Come on up, we'll show you a thing or two!

JONATHAN After me! God's put them at our mercy!

NARRATOR He scrambled up on his hands and knees, the young soldier after him. They caught the sentries by surprise (they had no idea there was a path up the cliff face). Jonathan knocked them down and his armour-bearer killed them off – twenty men on the narrow ledge.
Panic spread throughout the Philistine camp – and beyond. There happened to be an earthquake just at that moment too; the Philistine army and the raiding columns were terrified and the panic became a rout.

The Israelite look-outs in Gibeah were watching the Philistine camp and saw the soldiers suddenly scattering in all directions.

SAUL   Who's missing? Find out!

NARRATOR   Jonathan and his armour-bearer were missing at the roll-call. Saul and his men raced over to the fight. Everybody seemed to be fighting everybody else; it was complete chaos. Even the Israelites who had gone over to the Philistines and were serving with their army deserted and joined Saul and Jonathan. Men who had been hiding in the highlands came out and joined in the pursuit. So God rescued the Israelites that day.
Alan Dale, 'Winding Quest'

COMMENT   Jonathan was very daring and brave to have taken on such odds but he was convinced of God's help. We too must remember, when things go badly, that God is at hand ready to help.

PRAYER   *Psalm 44*
O God, we ourselves have heard –
our fathers have told us –
all you did in their days long ago:
uprooting and planting peoples,
hewing down and transplanting.
It wasn't our soldiers who conquered the country,
or our arms that won us the victory;
it was the strength of your hand and arm,
the light of your face –
your good favour.
In God we will boast all the day,
to your name for ever give thanks!

HYMN   *Father, I place into your hands.* HON 114, HONS 133, HONA 121
I will be with you. HON 188, HONS 263, CHB 104

D29 Friendship with God

OPENING RECORD *You've got a friend,* James Taylor. WB. *(Fade after 1 minute 30 seconds.)*

COMMENT It's a great shame when people stop talking to God as a friend. Many young people learn to pray and do it quite naturally when they are children, but think it is childish and drop it as they get older. Listen to this wonderful story of the closeness between Abraham and God; Abraham felt close enough to God to dare to argue and bargain with him.

READING

NARRATOR Using three messengers, God told Abraham what he was going to do.

GOD I have heard a cry for help against the two towns, Sodom and Gomorrah. I must go down to see what it's all about. I must know if their conduct is what I think it is.

NARRATOR God's messengers went on down towards the town; Abraham remained standing in God's presence. They were on the high hills and the valleys lay all below them.

ABRAHAM Would you sweep away the good people with the bad? Suppose there were fifty good people in the town, would you sweep it away – and not spare it for the sake of those fifty? I don't think you could do such a thing – treat good and bad alike. Must not the Judge of all the earth himself be just?

GOD I will spare the whole town if I find fifty good people living there.

ABRAHAM I am a mere man, and yet I dare to speak to you who are God. Suppose there aren't fifty; suppose there are five short? Will you sweep away the whole town just because there are five short?

GOD If I find forty-five good people in the town, I won't sweep it away.

ABRAHAM Suppose there are only forty?

GOD For the sake of forty, I will not sweep the town away.

ABRAHAM Don't be angry with me if I go on. Suppose the number is thirty?

GOD I will not do it if I find thirty.

ABRAHAM I am daring to speak again. Suppose there are only twenty?

GOD I will not sweep the town away for the sake of those twenty.

ABRAHAM Don't be angry with me for speaking again. Suppose only ten good people are to be found there?

GOD For the sake of those ten, I will not sweep it away.

NARRATOR   God had no more to say and went on his way; Abraham went home.
Alan Dale, 'Winding Quest'

COMMENT   Jesus said, 'Unless you become like little children, you shall not enter into heaven'. He meant that we should grow up, of course, but keep a simple trust and closeness to God our Father. Jesus taught us to think of God as a loving parent, with whom we can share all our worries and problems. God knows more about us than anyone else.

READING   I thank you for being what you are –
awe-inspiring, wonderful,
wonderful in all you do.
You made me the person I am
in the depth of my being;
you've known what I am really like
from the moment I was born.
You have watched the marvel of my body,
the wonder of my birth;
you've seen me grow up
and marked all I've done –
no day passed by uncounted,
slipped by unnoticed.

What you think of me matters to me, O God,
more than anything else –
how much you know about me!
I cannot fathom your thoughts
any more than I can count the sand on the shore!
Yet after all my searching
I am still in your presence!
Alan Dale, 'Winding Quest'

PRAYER   Remembering that we are now, this very minute, in God's presence, let us say the prayer that Jesus himself taught us to say.

Our Father . . .

HYMN   *If God is for us.* HON 192, HONS 231
When we walk with the Lord. HONA 553
or replay the opening record.

D30 Confidence in God

OPENING RECORD Theme music from *Star Wars*.

COMMENT Did you see *Star Wars* and the sequels? The heroes wished one another, 'May the Force be with you'. In the film they had a clear idea that they couldn't beat the power of Darth Vader, the power of evil, on their own; they needed the power of good on their side.

In the Bible, God sometimes asks people to do difficult and dangerous things. He says to them, 'I will be with you'.

READING

NARRATOR At Ophrah, in the Jezreel Plain, there was an oak tree. It belonged to a man called Joash whose son was called Gideon. The Midianites – camel-riding nomads from the desert – were raiding the Hebrew villages.

Gideon was threshing wheat, but not openly on the village threshing-floor. He was beating a few sheaves of wheat down on the floor of the wine-press, to keep it out of sight of the raiders. God spoke to him there.

GOD God is with you, brave hero.

GIDEON Then tell me, if God is on our side, why has there been all this raiding?

GOD You're a leader. Go and rescue your fellow countrymen from the raiders. Am I not sending you?

GIDEON Tell me, sir, how can I rescue my fellow countrymen? We're the poorest clan in Manasseh; and I carry no influence at all in my clan.

GOD I will be on your side. You shall wipe out the raiders to the last man.

GIDEON Don't go away, I beg you. Wait here till I come back with my present for you.

GOD I'll stay till you come back.

NARRATOR Gideon went inside. He prepared a kid-goat and made unleavened cakes with some flour. He put the meat in a basket and the broth in a pot. He brought them back to the oak tree and offered his present to his visitor. Gideon built an altar on the spot. He was filled with God's Spirit and mustered his clan to follow him. They got up early and set up camp near Harod Well. The raider's camp lay to the north of them, by Teacher's Hill in the valley of Jezreel.

That night God spoke to Gideon.

GOD Get up and go down to the camp. It's yours. If you are too scared to go alone, take your servant Purah with you. Listen to the raiders talking. That will give you courage enough to attack the camp.

NARRATOR They both crept down to the camp and got close to the tents of the outposts. A man was talking.

FIRST RAIDER I've just had a strange dream. I saw a loaf of barley bread come tumbling into the camp. It smashed a tent flat.

SECOND RAIDER   I know what that means. It's Gideon's army. It means we're beaten.

NARRATOR   When Gideon heard that, he said a prayer to God and went back to his own men.

GIDEON   Up! God's giving the raiders into our hands!

NARRATOR   He divided his three hundred men into three companies and gave them jars with torches inside.

GIDEON   Watch me. When we reach the tents, make sure you do just what I do. And when I blow the trumpet, shout, 'For God and for Gideon!'

NARRATOR   They reached the camp about midnight, just after the guard had been changed. They surrounded it, smashed the jars with a loud noise, waved the torches in their left hands and held their swords in their right hands.

ALL   For God and for Gideon!

NARRATOR   The camp awoke and stampeded down the valley and over the Jordan. Gideon had only three hundred men, but they followed the raiders across the Jordan and into the eastern highlands.

He followed the caravan road and caught the raiders off their guard. The chieftains escaped. He went after them and caught them; and the raiding army melted away. He turned for home.
Alan Dale, 'Winding Quest'

COMMENT   God is always with us, wherever we are. We can always ask him for help.

PRAYER   *Psalm 121*
God, guardian of his people,
is never drowsy or sleepy.
God is your guardian at your side.
No harm shall come to you
from the sun in the daytime,
from the moon at night.
God will guard your whole life
from every danger –
when you go out, and when you come home,
from now on and for ever!

HYMN   *Give me joy in my heart.* HON 135, HONS 159, HONA 153
Be still and know. HON 50, HONS 58, HONA 52
or bring up the theme music of *Star Wars* at the end of the prayer.

D31 Vocation

OPENING RECORD   *Search for the hero*, MPeople. The Best of MPeople. BMG. *(Last minute.)*

COMMENT   'Aim so high' and 'search for the secrets you hide' are the key words in this popular song. What you are called by God to do is there within you. Search your talents; listen for God's voice.

READING 1

NARRATOR   The boy Samuel was ministering to the Lord in the presence of Eli; it was rare for the Lord to speak in those days; visions were uncommon. One day, it happened that Eli was lying down in his room. His eyes were beginning to grow dim and he could no longer see. The lamp of God had not yet gone out and Samuel was lying in the sanctuary of the Lord where the Ark of God was, when the Lord called.

GOD   *(Voice offstage)* Samuel! Samuel!

NARRATOR   Samuel answered,

SAMUEL   Here I am.

NARRATOR   Samuel ran to Eli,

SAMUEL   Here I am, since you called me.

ELI   I did not call. Go back and lie down.

NARRATOR   So he went back and lay down. Once again the Lord called,

GOD   Samuel! Samuel!

NARRATOR   Samuel got up and went to Eli.

SAMUEL   Here I am, since you called me.

ELI   I did not call you, my son. Go back and lie down.

NARRATOR   Samuel had as yet no knowledge of the Lord, and the word of the Lord had not yet been revealed to him. Once again the Lord called, the third time.

GOD   Samuel! Samuel!

SAMUEL   *(to Eli)* Here I am, since you called me.

NARRATOR   Eli then understood that it was the Lord who was calling the boy.

ELI   Go and lie down, and if someone calls, say, 'Speak, Lord, your servant is listening.'

NARRATOR   So Samuel went and lay down in his place. The Lord then came, calling as he had done before,

GOD   Samuel! Samuel!

SAMUEL   Speak, Lord, your servant is listening.
1 Samuel 3:1-9 (Jerusalem Bible)

COMMENT   Samuel was surprised to be called by God. God often chooses the people we would least expect to work for him. Here is how Jeremiah the prophet remembered his calling by God:

READING 2

JEREMIAH   The word of the Lord was addressed to me, saying,

GOD   *(Voice offstage)*
Before I formed you in the womb I knew you;
before you came to birth I consecrated you;
I have appointed you as prophet to the nations.

JEREMIAH   I said, 'Ah, Lord; look, I do not know how to speak; I am a child!'

GOD   Do not say, 'I am a child'.
Go now to those to whom I send you
and say whatever I command you.
Do not be afraid of them,
for I will protect you –
it is the Lord who speaks!

JEREMIAH   Then the Lord put out his hand and touched my mouth and said to me:

GOD   There! I am putting my words into your mouth.
Look, today I am setting you
over nations and kingdoms,
to tear up and to knock down,
to destroy and to overthrow,
to build and to plant.
Jeremiah 1:4-10 (Jerusalem Bible)

RECORD   Bring up *Search for the hero*, then fade.

PRAYER   Almighty Father,
I would like to reach up and aim high.
Help me to search
for what you want me to do
with my life.
I wish I could be like Samuel
and hear you speaking to me.
Make my faith and trust deeper
that I may come closer to you.
May I always be open to your will for me;
just show me what it is. Amen.

HYMN   *All that I am, all that I do.* HON 19, HONS 28, HONA 19

D32 Respect for authority

OPENING RECORD   *Bridge over troubled waters*, Simon and Garfunkel. CBS. *(Fade after 1 minute 30 seconds.)*

COMMENT   When two people are at loggerheads it sometimes requires one to make the first move – to offer friendship or make some gesture of respect and regard. David did that when Saul was hunting him to kill him.

READING

NARRATOR   The people of Ziph took the news that David was hiding near them to Saul in Gibeah. He called out his crack troops and marched to the wilderness of Ziph to hunt David out. He pitched camp on Hachilah Hill on the road facing the desert.

   David was out in the rough moorlands when he heard that Saul was tracking him down. He sent scouts to find out where Saul was.

   Then he moved quickly, He marched by night to the outskirts of Saul's camp. Saul and his commander-in-chief, Abner, were asleep – Saul lying in the trench, the soldiers in their tents round him as a guard.

   David called two men, the Hittite Ahimelech and Abishai.

DAVID   Which one of you will go down with me to the camp, to Saul?

ABISHAI   I will.

NARRATOR   So, through the darkness, the two men stole down to the camp. There was Saul lying asleep in the trench, his spear stuck in the ground at his head, Abner and the soldiers lying round him.

ABISHAI   God has put your enemy at your mercy. I'll pin him to the earth with his own spear. One stroke's enough.

DAVID   No murder. Saul is God's anointed king. Murder of God's anointed king is a dreadful thing. In God's name, no murder! We'll leave him in God's hands, to die an ordinary death or meet a soldier's violent end. But God forbid that I should lay my hand on his anointed king. Get the spear at his head, and the water jug there – and let's get out!

NARRATOR   So they took the spear and the water jug from near Saul's head and slipped away. Nobody saw or heard them, and nobody woke up. They were all sound asleep. David crossed the valley and stood at a safe distance on a hilltop on the other side. He was so far off that he had to shout as loud as he could to be heard.

DAVID   Why don't you answer, Abner?

ABNER   Who are you, calling up the king like this?

DAVID   You're a fine soldier! You're the finest soldier of them all! What sort of guard is this to keep over His Majesty the King? Didn't you know there's an assassin prowling round? What a soldier you are! By God, you ought to be executed for sleeping; you're supposed to be on guard, you know! See where the king's spear and his water jug are now – not at his head!

NARRATOR   Saul, awake by now, recognised David's voice.

SAUL   Is that you, my son David?

DAVID   It is, your Majesty. And let me finish what I have to say. Why do you hunt me like this? What have I done wrong? If God has made you do this, let us ask his forgiveness; but if it's just slander, God's curse be on the slanderers – they have driven me out of the fellowship of God's people and tried to make me a foreigner. Don't let my blood be spilt in this foreign countryside. You're hunting me like a hawk hunting a partridge in the highlands!

SAUL   I'm in the wrong. Come back to me, my son David. I'll do you no more hurt; you treated me as the real king today. I've been a fool and done a dreadful thing.

DAVID   The king's spear is here. Let one of the soldiers come over and fetch it.

SAUL   God bless you, my son David. You've a great future in front of you!

NARRATOR   David went on his way and Saul went home.
Alan Dale, 'Winding Quest'

COMMENT   David could so easily have killed Saul the man who had been hunting him, but he had too great a respect for authority. Those who are in authority, whether it is in government, the police, school or home should remember that all authority springs from God. And God exercises his authority in loving care.

In the psalm of thanksgiving which follows, please reply, 'His love is everlasting' to each of the reader's invocations.

PRAYER
READER   After each phrase, please respond, 'His love is everlasting!'

Psalm 136
Give thanks to the Lord for he is good.
His love is everlasting!

Give thanks to the God of gods.
His love is everlasting!

Give thanks to the Lord of lords.
His love is everlasting!

He alone performs great marvels.
His love is everlasting!

His wisdom made the heavens.
His love is everlasting!

He set the earth on the waters.
His love is everlasting!

He made the great lights.
His love is everlasting!

The sun to govern the day.
His love is everlasting!

Moon and stars to govern the night.
His love is everlasting!

He provides for all living creatures.
His love is everlasting!

Give thanks to the God of heaven.
His love is everlasting!

Hymn   *All the nations.* HON 22, HONS 30, HONA 20
Praise him, praise him. HON 344, HONS 448, HONA 421
or replay opening record.

D33 Forgiveness

OPENING RECORD *Joseph and the Amazing Technicolor Dreamcoat.* Decca. *(Fade after 1 minute 40 seconds.)*

READING

NARRATOR Joseph was 17 years old. His father had been quite an old man when he was born, and he had always openly treated him as his favourite son. He made him a princely coat (a coat with long sleeves) to wear. His brothers resented all this; they hadn't a kind word to say to him.

Now Joseph used to dream and he could not keep his dreams to himself. This too upset his brothers. The time came for the brothers to lead the flocks away to the north to Shechem, to summer pastures. The grass was more abundant there than around Hebron. His father spoke to Joseph one day.

JACOB Your brothers are away in the highlands. I want you to go and visit them for me.

JOSEPH All right.

JACOB See how they and the sheep are getting on and bring me any news.

NARRATOR Joseph found his brothers near Dothan, an ancient Canaanite city. They saw him coming. Here was their chance to get their own back. By the time he'd got up to them, they'd made up their minds.

BROTHERS (TOGETHER) Here comes the dreamer! Let's get rid of him and throw his body into one of these rain-pits. We can make up a story about his being eaten by a wild animal. We'll make his dreams come true all right!

REUBEN Let's have no murder. Throw him into one of these rain-pits, if you want, but keep your hands off him.

NARRATOR He intended to come back and get him out of the pit and take him home.

They threw him into one of the empty rain-pits. Quite by chance, some Midianite traders passed by. They pulled the boy out of the pit and took him off to Egypt with them. Reuben came back to the pit – but there was no Joseph in it. He tore his clothes in grief and ran back to his brothers.

REUBEN The lad's gone! And now what am I to do? How can I go home?

NARRATOR The brothers had taken Joseph's fine long-sleeved coat off him before they threw him into the pit. They tore it up and took it home with them to their father.

BROTHERS We found this. Can you recognise it?

JACOB It's my son's cloak! A wild animal's mauled him. He must have been torn to pieces!

NARRATOR In his grief, Jacob tore his clothes and put sackcloth on. He broke down in tears.

COMMENT   Joseph, you remember, after being a servant for a short time, found himself in prison. He got out of prison by being able to interpret the Pharaoh's dreams. Pharaoh was so grateful that he made Joseph second-in-command in Egypt. Famine struck his family's homeland and the brothers came to Egypt begging for grain.

RECORD (OPTIONAL)   *Joseph and the Amazing Technicolor Dreamcoat.* 'Close every door'.

COMMENT   Joseph was released from prison when he successfully interpreted the Pharaoh's dreams. After playing a few tricks on the brothers, Joseph told them who he was.

READING

NARRATOR   Joseph could hold back his feelings no longer. He ordered all officials out of the audience room. Then he broke down – everybody in the palace could hear his weeping.

JOSEPH   Come near to me.

NARRATOR   The brothers gathered round him.

JOSEPH   I am your brother Joseph. Now don't be angry with yourselves for what you did. There are five more years of famine ahead of us; God sent me here so that our family might survive. You must go back home with this message from me to my father: 'God has made me Viceroy of Egypt. Make haste and come down to me. You can live in the land of Goshen, near me – you and the whole clan with your flocks and possessions. I will look after you and see that you don't starve.'
Alan Dale, 'Winding Quest'

COMMENT   What do we learn from this story? There are many lessons but one is the willingness to forgive. Joseph forgave his brothers for trying to kill him, and for the years he'd spent in prison. He bore no grudge.

PRAYER   Loving Father,
when we pray 'Forgive us our sins
as we forgive those who sin against us',
help us to remember Joseph's example.
May we experience the joy of restored relationships
as we forgive others
and you forgive us. Amen.

RECORD   *Joseph and the Amazing Technicolor Dreamcoat.* 'Close every door'.
(Last 2 minutes, fade.)

D34 Doing God's will

OPENING RECORD *Sailing,* Rod Stewart. WB. *(Fade after 1 minute.)*

COMMENT The usual way to sail is in a boat, but Jonah in the Old Testament found himself travelling in a great sea beast. (Many people believe that the story you are about to hear was made up to teach a truth – that God cares about everyone. Jonah, a Jew, did not want to go and talk to non-Jews – but God insisted!)

READING

NARRATOR Once upon a time God spoke to Jonah.

GOD Get up, and go to that great city, Nineveh. Pronounce its doom – its shameful wickedness has been reported to me.

NARRATOR Jonah set off – but he made for Tarshish in the far west, right away from God. He went down to the port of Joppa. There was a large cargo boat in the harbour. He paid his fare and went on board; he didn't want to have anything to do with God and his commands. Out at sea they ran into a hurricane. The sea was so rough that the ship seemed about to break up. The sailors were in a panic, each shouting out to his own god for help. They threw the cargo overboard to lighten the ship.

Jonah had gone down into the hold, and was lying there fast asleep. The captain went down to see what he was doing.

CAPTAIN What do you mean by sleeping like this? Get up and pray to your God. He might take some notice of us and come to our help.

NARRATOR Meanwhile the sailors were talking together.

FIRST SAILOR Let's toss up, and find out who's to blame for this bad luck.

NARRATOR They tossed up – it was Jonah!

SECOND SAILOR Tell us your business, where do you come from? What's your country? Who are your people?

JONAH I'm a Hebrew. I'm running away from God – the God of heaven who made the sea and the land.

FIRST SAILOR What a thing to do! What shall we do with you to quieten the storm?

NARRATOR The sea was growing rougher and rougher.

JONAH Throw me overboard. That will calm the sea. I know I am to blame for this hurricane.

NARRATOR But the men didn't throw him overboard. They rowed as hard as they could to get the ship into harbour. All in vain – the sea grew stormier and stormier still. Then they prayed to Jonah's God:

SAILORS   O God, don't let us die if we throw this man overboard; don't hold it against us. The storm is your doing.

NARRATOR   Then they threw Jonah overboard – and the storm died down. The sailors were filled with awe in God's presence; they worshipped him and vowed to serve him.

God sent a great fish. It swallowed Jonah, and there he stayed, inside the fish, for three whole days. God then ordered the fish to put Jonah on shore, and it vomited him out on to the dry land.
Alan Dale, 'Winding Quest'

COMMENT   The Bible story says that the storm arose because Jonah was going off in the opposite direction to the one God wanted him to take – he was running away from doing what God had asked. Eventually Jonah did as he was told.

PRAYER   *Psalm 145*
I sing your praises, God my King,
I bless your name for ever and ever,
blessing you day after day,
and praising your name for ever and ever.

Always true to his promises,
the Lord shows love in all he does.
Only stumble, and the Lord at once supports you;
if others bow you down, he will raise you up.

The Lord's praise be ever in my mouth,
and let every creature bless his holy name
for ever and ever.

HYMN   *Praise we our God with joy.* HON 350, HONS 458
Praise to the Lord, the Almighty. HON 348, HONS 456, HONA 427
or replay opening record.

D35 God's covenant

OPENING RECORD   *By the rivers of Babylon*, Boney M. Atlantic. *(Fade after 1 minute 30 seconds.)*

COMMENT   Powerful armies swept in from the north and overran the Jewish people and thousands of them were taken away into exile in Babylon. This exile had been threatened by the prophets because the Jews had failed to follow God's way.

READING   In the days that are to be, God says,
I will make a new covenant
with both North and South.

It won't be like the old covenant
I made on the desert march
when I led your ancestors out of Egypt.
That covenant was broken long ago –
That's why I said No to them.

This is the new covenant
I will make with the whole people:
my way shall be clear to everybody's conscience,
something every man can recognise;
I will really be their God,
they shall really be my people.

There'll be no need for teachers,
for anybody to say,
'Live in God's Way'
to neighbour or brother.
Each shall know for himself
what my way is – humble peasant
and king on his throne alike,
says God.

I'll forgive them
the wrong they've done – their disloyalty
shall be a thing of the past.
Alan Dale, 'Winding Quest'

COMMENT   God did make a new covenant with his people, but not before the Jews had suffered much unhappiness and had even been asked to sing their own religious songs for their guards.

READING   *Psalm 137*
Beside the streams of Babylon
we sat and wept
at the memory of Zion,
leaving our harps hanging on the poplars there.
For we had been asked
to sing to our captors,
to entertain those who had carried us off:

'Sing' they said
'some hymns of Zion.'
How could we sing
one of the Lord's hymns
in a pagan country?
Jerusalem, if I forget you
may my right hand wither!

RECORD   *By the rivers of Babylon. (The remainder of the record.)*

COMMENT   The agreement, or covenant, that God made with his People prepared a way for the coming of the Christ. Jesus, as our Lord and Christ, gave us a covenant – a new and lasting agreement.

READING   While they were at supper Jesus took some bread, and when he had given thanks, broke it and gave it to them saying, 'This is my body which will be given for you; do this as a memorial of me.' He did the same with the cup after supper, and said, 'This cup is the new covenant in my blood which will be poured out for you.' *Luke 22:19-20*

(Short period of silence)

HYMN   *Love is his word.* HON 258, HONS 338, HONA 322
or replay opening record.

WORLD RELIGIOUS THEMES

E36 Creation

OPENING RECORD Holst, *The Planets. (Suitable short extract.)*

COMMENT That piece of music is taken from *The Planets* by Holst. These days, when pictures are sent hundreds of millions of miles back in space from space probes from other planets in our solar system, it is natural to ask how this planet – Earth – got here. This question – where did Earth come from – has always puzzled man. All the religions of the world have stories about creation. Here are three.

READER A The holy men of ancient India often wondered how the universe was made. They were specially puzzled about how creation began. The first reading is from a book called *The Laws of Manu.*

The universe we live in was like darkness:
unnoticed, difficult to recognise, impossible
to understand; beyond knowledge;
like someone who is far away, or fast asleep.

Then he himself appeared, divine,
impossible to recognise:
the one who made it all –
the great things and the little things
that we can know, and learn about.
He himself appeared, with power you can't resist:
power to create.
He came, and the darkness faded away.
Laws of Manu 1.5.1

READER B The second reading is from the Muslim holy book, the *Qur'an.*

God is he who created the heavens and the earth and sent down water from the clouds, then brought forth with it the fruits as a sustenance for you, and he has made subservient to you the sun and the moon pursuing their courses, and he has made subservient to you the night and the day. And he gives you all that you ask him, and if you count God's favours, you will not be able to number them; surely man is very unjust, very ungrateful. *The Qur'an*

READER C The Jewish people too had their stories of creation. This is the first of the two that appear in the Bible. It is imagined how God spread the work of creation over seven days; here is a little of it.

This is the story of the making
of earth and sky:
in the very beginning,
God made them both.

Earth was formless chaos
lost in darkness
with stormy winds
sweeping over the vast waters.
'Let there be light!' said God –
and everywhere there was light,
splendid in his eyes.
He marked off light from darkness,
calling light 'day'
and darkness 'night':
so came the evening and the morning
of the first day.
Alan Dale, 'Winding Quest'

COMMENT These are religious ways of trying to understand that tremendous event – the beginning of life on planet earth. A modern poet tries to put the same ideas into the language of our day.

READER D And God stepped out on space,
and he looked around and said:
'I'm lonely . . .
I'll make me a world.'

As far as the eye of God could see
darkness covered everything
blacker than a hundred midnights
down in a cypress swamp.
Then God smiled
and the light broke,
and the darkness rolled up on one side,
and the light stood shining on the other,
and God said: 'That's good!'
James Weldon Johnson, 'The Creation'

COMMENT If you look into space on a clear night, and start to think about how far away the stars are; how many points of light you can see, whether space has an ending to it and so on – then you begin to realise the sheer vastness of it all. And the mighty power of God. We are so small before so great a wonder.

HYMN *Morning has broken.* HON 269, HON 350, HONA 337
For the beauty of the earth. HONA 137

E37 Supreme Being

OPENING RECORD *(as background music)* Beethoven, *Symphony No. 6,* 'Pastoral'. Philips. *(Short extract.)*

READING 1 *Psalm 8*
O God our king
how majestic you are!
Your glory is in the earth,
your splendour in the skies!
When I gaze at the sky
your fingers formed,
the moon and the stars
you have set there –
'What is man,' I cry,
'that you should notice him,
mortal man,
that you should care about him?'

COMMENT The idea of God – the Supreme Being – is common to most religions. He (or she) is mighty and powerful; the creator – as the Jews understood. The reading we have just heard is from the Hebrew Bible (what we call the Old Testament), one of the Jewish psalms found in the Bible.

    The Muslims have ninety-nine names for this Supreme Being. The Muslim faith reminds us that God has no beginning or end.

READING 2 'Say: God is one
the eternal God.
He begets not nor is he begotten
and there is none like him.'

COMMENT Those words are from the Muslim *Qur'an*. It also states:

READING 2
(continued) 'Say you: we believe in God and in that which has been sent down on us and sent down on Abraham, Ishmael, Isaac and Jacob and the tribes, and that which was given to Moses and Jesus and the prophets of the Lord. We make no division between any of them and to him we surrender.'

COMMENT For Hindus there are many gods but . . .

READING 3 'Whichever god you pray to, it is I who answer the prayer', says Krishna, who combines the concept of God and the Absolute.
    'As different streams, having different sources, all find their way to the sea, so, O Lord, the different paths which men take all lead to thee.'

COMMENT A modern poet reminds us that the awesome mystery of God is not only far above and beyond this world, but also within it.

READING 4 The emeralds are singing on the grasses
and in the trees the bells of the long cold are ringing.
My blood seems changed to emeralds
like the spears of grass beneath the earth piercing and singing.

The flame of the first blade
is an angel piercing through the earth to sing
'GOD is everything!'
The grass within the grass, the angel in the angel,
flame within the flame, and he is the green shade that came
to be the heart of shade.
The grey-beard angel of the stone,
who has grown wise with age, cried, 'Not alone
am I within my silence – God is the stone in the still stone,
the silence laid in the heart of silence . . .
then, above the glade the yellow straws of light
whereof the sun has built his nest, cry,
'Bright is the world, the yellow straw
my brother – God is the straw within the straw;
all things are Light.'

He is the sea of ripeness and the sweet apple's emerald lore.
So you, my flame of grass, my root of the world
from which all spring shall grow,
O you, my hawthorn bough of the stars, now leaning low
through the day, for your flowers to kiss my lips,
shall know
he is the core of the heart of love and he, beyond labouring seas,
our ultimate shore.
Edith Sitwell, 'How Many Heavens'

RECORD   *If available the following record fits well here.*
My sweet Lord, George Harrison. Apple.

or

HYMN   *O Lord, my God.* HON 311, HONS 404, HONA 380
Immortal, invisible. HON 196, HONS 242, HONA 242

E38 Worship

OPENING RECORD *Just for you*, MPeople. The Best of MPeople. BMG.

COMMENT Just for us God has created this beautiful world with its majestic mountains and awesome oceans. Jesus, just for us, sacrificed everything; he gave his own life; just for us.

Men and women of all ages have believed that if there is a Supreme Being then we owe him respect and worship. This is how a pagan Roman prayed.

READER A In his famous story of Rome, the Latin writer Livey tells how the Admiral of the Roman Fleet, Scipio Africanus, prayed as he prepared to attack the North African city of Carthage, in 204 BC.

I pray to all the gods and goddesses
who live on land or in the sea,
I pray you, with all my heart,
that what men have done already, under my orders,
will help me.

Give us the power to take revenge on our enemies:
give to me, and to the Roman people,
the power to do to Carthage
what they planned to do to us;
show them what it means to suffer punishment from God.
Donald G. Butler (ed.), 'Many Lights'

COMMENT Those were not Christian words or ideas. We can find the Christian approach to prayer in the Rule and Way of Life written by St Benedict for his monks, 1450 years ago.

READER B When we make requests to men in high positions,
we would not dare to do so without
respect and politeness;
even more, then, we should pray to God,
the Lord of All,
with politeness, and devout sincerity in our hearts.
We must realise that our prayers will be heard,
not if we just pray, over and over again,
but if we are really sincere,
and really sorry for our sins.
So prayers ought to be short and sincere
(unless we are really inspired to pray longer).
Donald G. Butler (ed.), 'Many Lights'

COMMENT The Hindu approach to worship is summed up in these words from the *Bhagavad-gita*.

READER C Fix your thoughts on me,
worship me, make offerings to me,
go down on your knee to me:

that is the way to get to know me.
Be sure of this: I promise:
I will not disappoint you:
you mean so much to me.
Donald G. Butler (ed.), 'Many Lights'

COMMENT Worship and prayer should be regular, as well as respectful. Regular daily prayer, praying five times a day, is an essential part of the Muslim faith.

READER D From the sacred book of Islam, the *Qur'an*, come these instructions about the right way for Muslims to say their daily prayers:

The five hours of prayer are –
In the early morning with a reading from the holy Qur'an;
immediately the sun begins to go down, after midday;
in the late afternoon;
immediately after sunset;
after the sun has set, and darkness has set in.
Donald G. Butler (ed.), 'Many Lights'

COMMENT Let us listen to and make our own the words of this song.

RECORD *Day by day*, Holly Sherwood. Bell.

or repeat the opening track, *or* sing

HYMN *I watch the sunrise.* HON 187, HONS 262
Lord Jesus Christ (Living Lord). HON 247, HONS 326, HONA 311

E39 Prayer

COMMENT A newspaper headline, 'Baboo, a man of peace who was kicked to death.'

READER A He was known as Baboo to his friends – easier to handle than Kayumarz Anklesaria, which even to his Pakistani compatriots was something of a mouthful.

Everyone who knew him has stories to tell about Baboo. They are all affectionate. For all are agreed he was the most gentle of men.

Yesterday Baboo was dead – the victim of a vicious, totally unprovoked, and possibly racially inspired attack on the London Underground.

He had left his home in Skelton Road, Forest Gate, London, at 4.45 pm on Thursday and gone by bus and Tube to a temple in West Hampstead to meditate and pray. At 11.53 pm as the train rolled into Bromley-by-Bow station, three white youths wearing brown lace-up, steel-capped, boots moved towards the doors. Suddenly, without any kind of warning, one delivered a savage Kung Fu-style kick at the Asian's neck. They ran out as the doors closed, laughing and shouting, and the train started to move.

Immediately a passenger pulled the emergency stop handle and the train jolted to a halt, still within the station. A group of nurses travelling on the train tried to make the injured man comfortable before an ambulance arrived to rush him to St Andrew's Hospital in Bow.

Baboo died of a smashed windpipe within half an hour of admittance.

Every week, as a devout Zoroastrian, he would travel across London to a converted temple in Compayne Gardens, West Hampstead. There he would burn sandalwood powder, and, kneeling before an open fire – the symbol of purity – he would pray to his god, Ahura Mazda, for peace, the love of his fellow man and for a world free of cruelty and violence.

When there was an earthquake in Turkey, in which thousands died, Baboo joined a volunteer organisation and, with only a sleeping-bag, went to help the refugees. He dug bodies from the rubble, helped the sick and injured.

That, say his friends, was the kind of man he was.

COMMENT A lot of you probably think that saying prayers is stuff for kids and young children, but not mature adults.

Baboo doesn't sound like an immature adult – but the sixteen-year-old who killed him certainly could not be called a mature, balanced person.

RECORD *A child's prayer,* Hot Chocolate. RAK.

COMMENT The children of the world's principal faiths all learn to pray.

READER B These are two of the prayers Jewish children say when they go to bed.

We bless you, Lord God, King of the Universe:
you draw the garments of sleep over my eyes,
you give my eyelids their gentle slumber.
May it please you, my Lord and God, the God of my family,
to allow me to go to rest in peace,
and to rise again tomorrow in peace.

We bless the Lord by day;
we bless the Lord by night;
we bless the Lord when we go to bed;
we bless the Lord when we wake up.
Donald G. Butler (ed.), 'Many Lights'

COMMENT   Sikh children learn to pray for those things which will help them most to live the life of a good Sikh.

READER C   God, grant me this prayer:
may I never turn away from the chance of doing good deeds.
May I never be afraid when I have to fight adversity.
May I never lose control when I win a victory.

I want, always, to have control over my heart.
This is what I want most from your goodness.

When the time finally comes for my life to find its end,
may I die in the thick of battles such as these.
Guru Gobind Singh, from Donald G. Butler (ed.), 'Many Lights'

COMMENT   The family prayer of the Christian family is the Lord's Prayer. Listen to this new translation.

READER D   Father in heaven,
we praise you:
we hold your honour in great respect.
You are our king
and you will be king in all the world.
Everyone here on earth will serve you,
as they do in heaven.
Give us day by day the food we need;
forgive the things that we do wrong,
as we forgive each other.
Help us when we are tempted to displease you;
protect us from every kind of evil power.
You are our king, powerful and glorious,
now and for ever.
Donald G. Butler (ed.), 'Many Lights'

RECORD   Replay *A child's prayer*, Hot Chocolate. RAK.

or

HYMN   *O Lord, all the world.* HON 309, HONS 403, HONA 378

E40 Fasting

OPENING RECORD   *Open your heart,* MPeople. The Best of MPeople. BMG. *(Use last 1 minute 35 seconds.)*

COMMENT   We need to open up our hearts to God and to the love of others. For hundreds of years the world religions have used fasting to help them to open up their hearts.

READER A   Abstention from food and drink on special occasions is practised for religious purposes. Many religions encourage their members to go without food and drink on special fast days and in preparation for religious festivals. In this way they remind their members that there is more to life than material things – like food and drink. We have a spiritual side to us as well. *Anon*

COMMENT   The Jews observe total fasting on their special day, the Day of Atonement; that is from sunset to sunset. The Muslims fast for a whole month. Let us listen to this account of the Muslim fast as it is kept in the Arab State of Kuwait.

READER B   The fast of Ramadhan begins with the sightseeing of the new moon after the sun goes down. The fast of Ramadhan is strictly observed in Kuwait and greatly affects the daily life of every Muslim and even non-Muslims. The fasting begins early in the morning when the 'white thread of day' appears on the horizon and ends at sunset, when people can eat as much as they wish until early next morning. In the morning they fast again. During Ramadhan Muslims may not drink, eat or smoke during daylight hours and this routine affects foreign Muslims and non-Muslims, who are expected out of politeness to refrain from smoking, drinking and eating in public.
Mgr. Victor Sanmiguel, 'Pastor in Kuwait'

COMMENT   From the very early days of Christianity, following the example of Jesus, who went out into the desert to fast, the Christian Church has always encouraged its members to abstain from food and drink, especially in preparation for the festivals of Christmas and Easter.

READER C   The Christian concept of fasting is somewhat different from that of the Muslims. During the Ramadhan, after dark, that is between sunset and sunrise, the Muslims are freely allowed to eat in quantity and quality according to their will. While Christians during Lent and other fasting days, in imitation of the fast of Christ in the desert, abstain themselves throughout the fasting, in quantity and quality, meditating on the Passion of Christ.

The purpose of the fasting, besides the sacrifice, is to moderate the sensual passions and general submission of the material to the spiritual and moral sphere of the life of the human person. This rule is good not only for those who profess the religious life, but also for the ordinary good Christian. *Anon*

COMMENT   Fasting, for a religious purpose, is of no value unless it is aimed at helping us to open up our hearts and help us to grow in our love for God and our neighbour.

CLOSING RECORD   *All you need is love,* The Beatles *(if available)*

or

HYMN   *Love is his word.* HON 258, HONS 338, HONA 322
Look around you. HON 241, HONS 316

E41 The Golden Rule

OPENING RECORD   *Colour my life,* MPeople. The Best of MPeople. BMG.

COMMENT   From time to time we are reminded by a pop group, or in a new slogan, that love is necessary for life, that it colours our life. If we love, our lives take on colour and interest. That is something that the religions of the world have been teaching for a very long time. It's called 'The Golden Rule'.

READER A   Jews and Christians, throughout the centuries, have not always been friends. Here is a story of the Golden Rule in action.

The Grand Rabbi of Lyons was a Jewish chaplain to the French army in the First World War. One day a wounded man staggered into a trench and told the Rabbi that a Roman Catholic was on the point of death, between the heavy guns, in no-man's-land. The soldier was begging that his priest would come to him with a crucifix. The Catholic padre could not be found. The Jewish rabbi rapidly made a cross with two pieces of wood, clambered out of the safety of the trench and ran out with it into no-man's-land and was seen to hold it before the dying man's eyes. He was almost immediately shot by a sniper; the bodies of the Catholic and the Jew were later found lying together.
Victor Gollancz

COMMENT   For hundreds of years Sikhs and Muslims have been enemies, with only a few to remind them of the Golden Rule.

READER B   During a battle between Muslims and Sikhs, a Sikh water carrier called Ghanaya was seen giving water to wounded Muslim soldiers as they lay suffering from thirst under the hot sun. He was brought to the Sikh spiritual leader, Guru Gobind Singh, and accused of being a traitor. The Guru heard the charges and asked Ghanaya to answer them.

'When I walked through the battlefields I saw no Muslims and no Sikhs, only your face in every man,' said Ghanaya.

'You are a true Sikh,' said the Guru. 'Continue the work; and here is some ointment to put on the wounds. You shall be known as Bhai Ghanaya from now on.' *Bhai* means brother; it is a term of honour among Sikhs, reserved for the best of men.
W. Owen Cole

COMMENT   It is interesting how close in thought the major religions of the world are when it comes to the wording of the Golden Rule to be found in their teaching.

READER A   The Hindu religion says: 'The true rule is to guard and do by the things of others as you do by your own.'

READER B   The Muslim faith says: 'Let none of you treat your brother in a way he himself would dislike to be treated.'

READER C   The Buddhist religion says: 'One should seek for others the happiness one desires for oneself.'

READER D   Jesus summed it up for the Christian, telling his followers to 'love one another as I have loved you'.

COMMENT   Let us close by reminding ourselves of our opening track; our lives will be 'colourful' if we are loving people. Now we can sing the song which was specially written for Christian Aid. In May, Christians all round Britain collect and raise money for their neighbours in the world who are poor and needy, no matter what their religion.

HYMN   *When I needed a neighbour.* HONA 548, CHB 229
Make me a channel of your peace. HON 262, HONS 342, HONA 328

E42 Festival of light

COMMENT Have you heard the story of the teacher who told the science class about the fantastic speed at which light travels? 'Isn't it wonderful,' said the teacher, 'to think of light coming to us from the sun at the speed of all those miles per second!'
'Not really,' one boy said, 'it's downhill all the way!'

Of course, light from the sun is essential to life on this planet – no sunlight, no life! Some world religions celebrate the importance of light and use it as a symbol in worship.

READER A The Jewish people have a special festival called *Hanukkah* which means *dedication*. On that day they celebrate the rededication of their temple in the year 165 BC. The Romans had allowed a Syrian king to turn the Jewish Temple into a place of worship for Greek pagan gods. A guerrilla leader called Judas the Hammer (Judas Maccabaeus) organised a revolt and his fighting men won back the Temple.

Judas the Hammer wanted to light a lamp as a sign of God's presence and love, but all the lamps had been damaged except one. This lamp only had enough oil in it for one day, but Judas lit it and was surprised when it burned for eight days.

The festival of Hannukkah lasts for eight days and, on a special eight-branched candlestick, one candle is lit each day.

READER B The Hindu religion has the *Feast of Lamps* or *Diwali*, when candles are lit in the window of each Hindu house. The festival lasts for three days, and houses have to be made clean and spotless. The light burning in each house, and the bigger fires built on the third day, are to remind the Hindus as they start a new year that, as light overcomes darkness, we must all struggle to overcome evil.

COMMENT Christianity also uses light as a symbol.

READER C The newly baptised person, child or adult, is given a lighted candle at the end of the Baptism service. This is to remind them that now they too, like Christ, must be a light in the world.

READER D The Easter Candle is blessed at the Easter service called the Easter Vigil, and stands in a prominent place in the church near the altar. This is to remind everyone that Christ is alive and risen.

HYMN *Lord, the light of your love is shining.* HON 253, HONA 317, CHB 148
The Light of Christ. HON 401, HONS 529

E43 Judgement

OPENING RECORD   *Bright eyes*, Art Garfunkel. *(Fade after 1 minute.)*

COMMENT   At some time or other all of you must have seen on TV the old films *The Mummy* or *The Mummy's Curse;* stories about finding secret passages and vaults in the pyramids and the burial riches of Pharaohs like Tutankhamen. Later in the story comes the effect of the legendary curse of the Pharaohs on those who tampered with their tombs.

The tombs were filled with treasures because the ancient Egyptians believed in a life after death. Their family and friends thought they would need all sorts of things in the next life. The Egyptians believed in many gods, but they also believed a person's soul was sent for judgement and his or her life was also examined. He was rewarded or punished according to how he'd lived.

READER A   I believe with all my heart,
that God knows everything that
his children do,
everything that they think.
As it says: he made all their hearts,
he knows all their deeds.

I believe with all my heart
that God
rewards those who keep his laws
and punishes those who break them.
Donald G. Butler (ed.), 'Many Lights'

COMMENT   Muslims too believe that there will be a judgement.

READER B   When a man dies, Muslims believe that he must undergo judgement. He may be condemned to hell or rewarded with heaven. Or he may be a very special person, and have a place very near to Allah's throne.

When the event inevitable
cometh to pass,
then will no soul
entertain falsehood
concerning its coming.
Many will it bring low;
many will it exalt.
Donald G. Butler (ed.), 'Many Lights'

COMMENT   If you have read *Watership Down* you will remember that when the good rabbit, Hazel, dies, the story tells how he goes to his reward with the rabbits' god. He had lived a good life so presumably he was going to live for ever in happiness. I wonder what happened to the baddy, General Woundwort, at death?

Christian belief in judgement at death is summed up in a short poem, written over 1,200 years ago by Bede, an Anglo-Saxon scholar.

RECORD   Play part of *Bright eyes (fade into the reading).*

READER C There is a journey ahead
for every one of us.

Before we begin that journey
we must, each one of us
(and none of us is so wise
that he can be left out),
think out, in good time,

what judgement his soul will get
after death.
Will it be a judgement of evil;
or a judgement of good?
Donald G. Butler (ed.), 'Many Lights'

PRAYER All that we ought to have thought and have not thought,
all that we ought to have said and have not said,
all that we ought to have done and have not done,
all that we ought not to have thought and yet have thought,
all that we ought not to have spoken and yet have spoken,
all that we ought not to have done and yet have done,
for these words and works pray we, O God,
for forgiveness,
and repent with penance.
'The Zendavesta', ascribed to Zoroaster, about 700 BC.

HYMN *Lord, for tomorrow.* HON 245, HONS 322
Dear Lord and father of mankind. HON 104, HONS 116, HONA 106

or close with *Bright eyes.*

E44 Heaven

COMMENT Have you ever dreamt of digging up buried treasure? People with metal detectors have made many finds, hoards of coins and jewellery, for example. Lots of interesting things from the past have been dug up. Not just hoards of coins and jewellery but important archaeological finds that help us to piece together how people used to live. Evidence of their beliefs has also come to light in the same way.

READER A The following poem was found on an earthen tablet about thirty years ago by archaeologists excavating the ancient city of Babylon. The tablet was very weathered and damaged.

READER B There stands a house under the mountain of the world,
a road runs down, the mountain covers it
and no man knows the way. It is a house
that binds bad men with ropes
and clamps them into a narrow space.
It is a house that separates the wicked
and the good; this is a house from out of which
no one escapes, but good people need not fear before its judge,
for in this river of spent souls the good
shall never die although the wicked perish.

COMMENT Those thoughts were put on the tablet about 600 years before Christ. That is over 2,500 years ago. Notice how the poet says 'the good shall never die'. The beliefs of Christians and Muslims continued this concept and gave more meaning and depth to the idea of heaven.

READER C Christians and Muslims affirm that there exists an Abode of Reward, Paradise, and an Abode of Punishment, Hell, though they differ widely in the descriptions they give of these places and in their understanding of what constitutes their essential elements. Does not Jesus announce in the Gospel that 'those who did good will rise again to life; and those who did evil to condemnation' (John 5:28-9)? Islamic tradition recognises the existence of 'pleasures of the mind and the senses', often interpreted metaphorically, and would seem to confine the 'vision of God' to a few rare moments and to the 'nearest amongst the elect'.
Mgr. Victor Sanmiguel, 'Pastor in Kuwait'

COMMENT The Irish people, converted by St Patrick, had a strong interest in both heaven and hell in the Middle Ages. Our assembly could end with *Be Thou my vision*, words which come from eighth-century Ireland.

HYMN *Be thou my vision.* HON 53, HONS 61, HONA 56

E45 Happy New Year

PREPARATIONS   *Five posters or placards are made with the following dates on one side and the religion on the other. They are carried by five pupils who stand up and show their poster **when** the content is mentioned (not before), first the side with the name of the world faith on, then the side with the date.*

Zoroastrian New Year	27 August
Jewish New Year	13/14 September (changes each year)
Hindu New Year	11 November
Christian New Year	Last Sunday of November or first of December
Muslim New Year	(the appropriate date for the year)

(Most world religions use a lunar calendar so dates need to be checked.)

COMMENT   On 1 January we go round saying 'Happy New Year'. A new calendar year begins. The world's religions, however, have their own New Year days.

READER A   The Zoroastrian New Year begins on 27 August. It is called Shanenshai. Listen now to a hymn of praise sung at that time.

READER B   Wise Lord, Lord of great thoughts:
judge my life.
Give me the success I deserve
in the two kinds of life I lead:
first in the things that I do,
and in the things that happen to me;
and secondly, in the thoughts that I think,
and in the peace of my mind.
In both of these, please
guide and help me,
and make me happy for ever.

READER A   The Jewish New Year begins about 13/14 September *(adapt for the year)* and is called Rosh Hashanah.

READER C   During the service in the synagogue that morning, the ram's horn is blown, to proclaim God as King of the Universe. This day celebrates God's creation of the universe. It marks the start of ten days of penitence.

READER A   The Hindu New Year begins on 11 November, or rather at a day fixed by tradition in October/November. The festival is called *Diwali*.

READER D   This is the Indian New Year festival of lights when lamps are ceremonially lit, house fronts are illuminated and gifts exchanged. Lakshmi, the goddess of prosperity, is believed to visit the homes lit by many lamps.

READER A   The Christian New Year begins on the first Sunday of Advent, which is either the last Sunday in November or the first in December.

READER E On the first day of Advent, the Advent wreath and calendar begin. If a wreath is being used, the first of four candles is lit or in homes that have the Advent calendar the first 'door' is opened. Both are step-by-step preparations for the great festival of Christ's birth.

READER A The Muslim New Year changes from year to year.

READER F The prophet Muhammad moved from Mecca to Medina in the year AD 622. There he organised his followers into a religious movement. The Muslim New Year begins with a celebration of the Prophet's action.

(Five pupils still hold the New Year dates to view.)

COMMENT Different world religions begin their religious new year at different points in our year. *(Pupils turn placards to show name of world faith – then leave together.)* Wish your Jewish friends 'Happy New Year' in September, your Hindu friends 'Happy New Year' in November, your Christian friends in December, your Muslim friends whenever their New Year falls, and together let us wish each other a Happy New calendar year on 1 January.

PRAYER Father Almighty,
you made us to be happy,
to be one with you;
but when sin entered the world
that happiness was frustrated.
We all long to be happy,
but it is all too easy to look for it
in the wrong places.
Please help each of us to seek happiness
through kindness and service to others.
We ask this through Christ your Son. Amen.

HYMN *Give me joy in my heart.* HON 123, HONS 159, HONA 153
Rejoice in the Lord always. HON 352, HONS 462, HONA 430

FAMILY AND PEOPLE GROUPS

F46 The family

ROLE-PLAY *(Two members of staff and one pupil, or three pupils, are needed.)*
Mother and father are sitting in armchairs (or simulated armchairs) watching TV – father reading newspaper at same time, mother doing the ironing.

FATHER   Look at that time! It's not good enough!

MOTHER   Well, it's only the second time – and he is 14 now.

FATHER   Yes – the second time this week!

(Enter son or daughter)

FATHER   Where do you think you've been!

BOY   *(placidly)* Out with my friends.

FATHER   Do you know what time it is? What do you think this place is – a hotel?

BOY   It's only just 11 o'clock, Dad.

FATHER   But I told you to be in at 10!

BOY   I said I might be a bit later – my friends don't have to be in until 11.

FATHER   I don't care what your friends do – you're grounded! You can forget about going out next week.

BOY   Tell him, Mum; it's not fair. I'm not really late.

MOTHER   Would you like a hot drink?

BOY   *(goes out slamming the door)* No, I'm going to bed.

COMMENT A scene which, I'm sure, is familiar to a lot of you. A famous Roman writer named Pliny once said, 'Home is where the heart is'. It's not that our hearts are not in our homes – we do love our family – but we feel that we need to stand on our own two feet. We need to develop independence. Somehow we have got to balance the love we have for our family, and respect for our parents, with a growing sense of responsibility for ourselves. Most people only learn to appreciate home and family properly when they become more mature. The following is taken from an interview with Roy Castle, the TV celebrity, conducted just months before he died a few years ago.

READING I realise that meeting and marrying Fiona was just the best thing that could have happened to me. For, quite apart from having given me four beautiful children, she gives me emotional security. And believe me, for a guy whose job it is to make people laugh, that's very important. Because security is the one thing most comedians find scarce. You never know from one minute to the next whether you're going to be loved or hated, cheered or booed. And that's enough to turn the sanest guy neurotic.

Fiona and the kids make me feel that, whatever the future holds for me, I'll always be wanted and loved. I was talking to an entertainer recently who told me he had made a conscious decision to concentrate on becoming a super-star at the expense of his family. For years he sought the limelight and the big time, and hardly spent any time at home. Finally, when he got home his two daughters were well into their teens. The bloke turned round to me and with deep regret in his voice admitted that the girls were total strangers to him.

And I thought to myself – what a waste. For no matter what you say, fame and fortune count for nothing compared to your own flesh and blood. What I've got is far more important than power. And it's peace of mind. The one commodity in life you can't ever over-estimate.

PRAYER Heavenly Father,
you love and care for us as members of your family.
Our parents love and care for us.
Please help us
when we disagree with our parents' point of view –
when we think they are being unreasonable.
Help us to try to see their point of view
and realise that they want to protect us from danger.
May we grow to true maturity and personal responsibility
but without hurt and damage to others.
We ask this through Christ your Son. Amen.

HYMN *A new commandment.* HON 1, HONS 39, HONA 4
God is love. HON 148, HONS 178, HONA 169

F47 Immigrants

OPENING RECORD   *Someday,* MPeople. The Best of MPeople. BMG.

COMMENT   'Someday, we'll live as one family.' That is the hope of all immigrants looking for a place to live. Over the centuries hundreds of thousands of people have come into the British Isles to settle down and make their home here.

READER A   The Saxons arrived on the eastern shores of our country, and drove the Celts out across England towards Wales and the West Country.

READER B   The Vikings came as raiding parties in their long boats; they stole and murdered but eventually many stayed and made their home in this country.

READER C   The Normans invaded and brought with them their French ways and language. The Saxon English resented them.

READER D   We had kings and queens of German blood who brought their people and customs with them.

READER E   Over the centuries Jewish traders and merchants came and settled; especially when they were expelled from their own native countries such as Russia and Germany.

READER F   The Irish came looking for work or driven out of their island by famine and oppressive landlords.

READER G   The British Empire spread and the Union Jack was the flag of the Colonies; English was their language and Victoria was their queen. From the Colonies and the Commonwealth they came to see their motherland and many made it their home.

COMMENT   Most of the modern inhabitants of this country have come originally from other lands.

READER A   In my classroom there are people from all nations, all over the world, some from Jamaica, some from Hong Kong. I don't care, they're all friends to me. From the hot countries to the cold countries and from black to white, we're all friends in our classroom. Our class can prove to all prejudiced people, all over the world, that people from different nations can live together. My background is a cold place called Britain. It is cold in the winter and warm in the summer, but not hot like in the other countries of America, India, Africa. The only difference between our countries is colour and language, and that's nothing really; we are all human and we can all show friendship and love for each other, and not war and hate between our colours.
Tommy Robertson

SCRIPTURE READING   Your trust in God your Father has made you members of his family; Jesus has made this possible. For when you were baptised and became friends of Jesus, you began, with his help, to live in his way – as he lived in his Father's way. Living in God's way means that you can't talk about one another as being

'white' or 'coloured', 'working class' or 'upper class', 'men' or 'women' – as though that were the only thing about them that matters. The most important thing is that as Christians you are one company of friends. *Galatians 3:26-29.*
Alan Dale, 'New World'

PRAYER Almighty God,
we know that you love everyone
and have no favourites.
Help us to be like you,
to treat everyone with care and kindness,
especially those we find it difficult to get on with.
We ask you this through your Son, Jesus,
who died for everyone
regardless of their colour or creed. Amen.

HYMN *One bread, one body.* HON 334, HONS 744
Jesus, stand among us. HONA 279

F48 Refugees

OPENING RECORD *By the rivers of Babylon,* Boney M. Atlantic.

COMMENT That song is based upon a song or psalm that the Jews composed while in exile – like refugees – in a foreign land. What are refugees?

READER A Because we rarely see refugees in our country, it is not easy for us to realise what a large number there are in the world today. As we read and listen to these words there are many hundreds of thousands of ordinary people, just like us, in different countries around the world, who have had to run away from their homes and become refugees.

In time of war, thousands become refugees; in time of political unrest, thousands leave their homes and try to find peace, safety and security elsewhere. Every time you hear of fighting and war on the TV news, there will be hundreds of people trying to get away from the troubled areas. Often they can never go back to their homes – they become refugees.

COMMENT Organisations like the Red Cross, the United Nations and Christian Aid try to help refugees. They need:

PUPIL 1 Food – because their crops are destroyed by bombing, tanks and all the mess-up of war.

PUPIL 2 Shelter – their homes are left behind and often destroyed or used for military purposes.

PUPIL 3 Medical care – travel and hardship affect especially the very young and the very old.

PUPIL 4 Loving care – for God said, 'Love your neighbour.'

READER B If a stranger lives with you in your land, do not molest him. You must count him one of your own countrymen and love him as yourself – for you were once strangers yourselves in Egypt. *Leviticus 19:33, 34*

COMMENT Not only the Jewish people but Jesus himself was once a refugee.

READER C After the Wise Men had left, the angel of the Lord appeared to Joseph in a dream and said, 'Get up, take the child and his mother with you, and escape into Egypt and stay there until I tell you, because Herod intends to search for the child and do away with him'. So Joseph got up and, taking the child and his mother with him, left that night for Egypt.
Matthew 2:13-15

COMMENT There's a song called *No turning back*. Let us use the words in a response litany. After each verse please answer:

It's a long, long road;
no time to pack.
Keep travelling on;
no turning back.

READER A Remember the people of Israel
tramping the desert sands;
hungry, anxious and weary,
looking for the Promised Land:

It's a long, long road;
no time to pack.
Keep travelling on;
no turning back.

Herod's soldiers came hunting
a king that was to be,
but Mary and Joseph took Jesus
to Egypt as a refugee.

It's a long, long road;
no time to pack.
Keep travelling on;
no turning back.

Foxes have holes to hole up in.
Birds can fly home to bed,
but the Son of Mary (said Jesus)
has nowhere to lay his head.

It's a long, long road;
no time to pack.
Keep travelling on;
no turning back.

Today there are families wandering,
parents and children too.
No homes, no clothes, no schooling,
and they've got no work to do.

It's a long, long road;
no time to pack.
Keep travelling on;
no turning back.

All they want is somewhere
that's free from fear and pain,
and a chance so they are able
to live in peace again.

It's a long, long road;
no time to pack.
Keep travelling on;
no turning back.

COMMENT Let us pray the prayer of St Francis (see below) or sing the song version,
Make me a channel of your peace, HON 262, HONS 342, HONA 328.

PRAYER Lord,
make me an instrument of your peace;
where there is hatred, let me sow love;
where there is injury, pardon;
where there is discord, union;
where there is doubt, faith;
where there is despair, hope;
where there is darkness, light;
where there is sadness, joy.
Attributed to St Francis of Assisi

F49 Travelling people/gypsies

COMMENT   Comments from a local paper: 'Pity the people of Dunton Green, on whom the gypsies have descended with their attendant piles of rubbish . . . it is difficult to stimulate the milk of human kindness towards gypsies in some of the desecrated areas with which we are all familiar. The sight of a roadside encampment is always a shock to the senses – no matter how often one sees it.'

ROLE-PLAY   *Village shop, woman serving from behind the counter, two villagers in shop, one being served, the other waiting. In walks a gypsy (could be man or woman). Behind the counter there is a sign which says, 'NO GYPSIES SERVED'.*

Talking in the shop stops. Shopkeeper looks at the gypsy then points, without a word, to the sign. Gypsy ignores her action.

Customer at the counter turns and says , 'Can't you read?'

Gypsy says, 'Yes, but I only wanted a bag of sugar.'

There follows an ad lib scene in which the gypsy argues that he (she) is human like anyone else – his money carries same value, and so on. The second customer accuses the shopkeeper of being 'a little unfair'. Scene finishes after a few minutes, once essential points have been made, with the shopkeeper saying, 'I'm calling the police' and the gypsy walking out of the shop.

READER A   The only possible solution to this most difficult problem is the establishment of properly planned and supervised sites for 'travelling families' as they are more generally known now.

READER B   It is estimated that there are over 7,000 travelling families in England and Wales. Since 1970, when the government passed the Caravan Site Act, only 160 sites have been established. That means two out of three gypsy families have no pitch on an official site. £30 million would have to be found to settle them. So far the money has not been found!

PRAYER   Please reply to each invocation:
'Happy are the poor in spirit;
theirs is the kingdom of heaven.'

We pray for those
who feel unwanted in our community,
especially the 7,000 travelling families.

*Happy are the poor in spirit;
theirs is the kingdom of heaven.*

We pray for those in our community
who cannot read and write properly,
especially for those among the travelling families.

*Happy are the poor in spirit;
theirs is the kingdom of heaven.*

We pray for those who are always being moved on
from one place to another,
especially the travelling families.

Happy are the poor in spirit;
theirs is the kingdom of heaven.

We pray for those who close their hearts
to those in need and develop prejudice,
especially against the travelling families.

Happy are the poor in spirit;
theirs is the kingdom of heaven.

We pray for our government
and those who can improve the lot of the 7,000 travelling families.

Happy are the poor in spirit;
theirs is the kingdom of heaven.

HYMN   *Whatsoever you do.* HON 452, HONS 606
Brother, sister, let me serve you. HONA 73, CHB 27

F50 The hungry

COMMENT	*(Six pupils sit on stage, or assembly area, in a line, facing the rest; between the fifth and sixth pupil there is a space.)*
	There is great hunger in the world. For every one of us who has enough to eat *(the sixth pupil stands up)* there are five who go to bed hungry every night *(the remaining five stand up).*
SIXTH PUPIL	*(Speaking to the assembled gathering.)* We've got a colour TV set in every bedroom now and I've just got a new computer.
FIFTH PUPIL	My family lives on the pavement in the city of Calcutta and we're lucky if we get one meal a day.
SIXTH PUPIL	My dad's just got a new car; it can do 120 miles an hour!
FOURTH PUPIL	My family, there's eight of us, live in a one-roomed hut of corrugated iron in Lima; that's in Peru. We're lucky if we get one meal a day.
SIXTH PUPIL	We're going on a family holiday to Florida this summer; we'll hire a car and visit Disney World and Universal Studios.
THIRD PUPIL	My dad left the family to try and find work in the city of Manila; he never came back, but sometimes my brothers and sisters beg a few coins from tourists; then we have a meal that day.
SIXTH PUPIL	I really like to be in fashion. My mother bought me some new Nike trainers the other day, they cost £80.
SECOND PUPIL	I'm really lucky, I've got a job in a factory making trainers. If I work hard all day from six in the morning to eight at night I make 220 pairs of trainers. I get paid enough for my family to have a meal that day.
SIXTH PUPIL	We had a collection at school today for CAFOD; you know, for the poor. Well, I mean I can't spare anything so I put in a handful of coins we had over from our holiday last year in Spain. They were no good to me.
FIRST PUPIL	We don't want your scraps and left-overs! We have our own dignity; we will help ourselves. If you could find it in your hearts to give us the tools and the seeds, we will do the planting.
COMMENT	There's no doubt about it, everyone in this room (or hall) is rich compared with most people in our world.
READING VOICE 1	*(Using different pupils)* Whose are the voices crying, crying? Whose are the pitiful pleas we hear? Whose is the sorrow that finds tongue in weeping? Whose hopelessness speaks with despair?

VOICE 2   Ours are the voices crying, crying;
           ours are the pitiful pleas you hear.
           We are the people you hear at our weeping.
           Ours is the empty cry of despair.

VOICE 1   Whose are the faces so drawn with suffering?
           Whose are the bodies no more than bones?
           Whose are the eyes that are hopeless and lifeless?
           Whose are the graves with nameless stones?

VOICE 2   Ours are the faces gaunt with starvation.
           Ours are the wasted dying frames.
           Ours are the hungry eyes of the hopeless.
           Ours are the graves with no names.

VOICE 1   Why do I hear your cries of starvation?
           Why show me hunger I don't wish to see?
           Why are your skeleton fingers still reaching
           endlessly, endlessly out to me?

VOICE 2   Have we been changed so much by our suffering?
           In our extremity aren't we the same?
           Brother to brother, we reach out our hands to you.
           Flesh of one flesh are we, name of one name.

VOICE 1   What can I do for you, brother, my brother?
           How can I help? I am too far away.
           Leave it to God, hungry brother, my brother.
           Go down on your thin starving knees, and pray.

VOICE 2   We have prayed, distant brother, with fierce desperation.

VOICE 1   Has God in his mercy shown what you must do?

VOICE 2   He has, brother, answered our earnest entreaties;
           he has answered our prayers and his answer is YOU.
           Anon

COMMENT   Do you remember the words of Jesus when he said that whatever we do to
           another person we do to him. So note, and note carefully, if we ignore the
           hungry, we ignore Christ – but if we help them, we help him.

SCRIPTURE READING   I was hungry and you gave me food;
           I was thirsty and you gave me drink;
           I was a foreigner and you took me home with you;
           I was in rags and you gave me clothes;
           I fell ill and you looked after me;
           I was in prison and you came to see me.
           Believe me –
           when you helped the least of my brothers and sisters,
           you helped me.

Assemble Together

I was hungry and you gave me no food;
I was thirsty and you gave me no drink;
I was a foreigner and you didn't take me home with you;
I was in rags and you gave me no clothes;
I fell ill and you didn't look after me;
I was in prison and you never came to see me.
Believe me –
when you didn't help the least of my brothers,
you didn't help me. *Matthew 25:31-46.*
Alan Dale, 'New World'

HYMN *The Lord hears the cry of the poor.* HON 401, HONS 765
When I needed a neighbour. HONA 548, CHB 229

F51 Elderly people

ROLE-PLAY/READING *Two pupils (boy and girl preferably) required as Mr and Mrs Phillips (in early 80s), another as the local social worker. Three or four 'off-stage' voices needed. Old couple sitting at kitchen table having breakfast.*

MR PHILLIPS *(reading a letter)* 'A car will take you to your local railway station and you will be met at Great Yarmouth station by a taxi which will take you to the hotel.'

MRS PHILLIPS I can't really believe it – our first holiday for ten years. And free, too. I can't believe it.

MR PHILLIPS *(laying down the letter and picking up a piece of toast.)* That social worker was right. I never thought we would qualify for a free holiday – I suppose being over 80 helps!

(There's the sound of breaking glass and half a house-brick lands on the table, smashing and scattering the table things. Mrs Phillips screams and slumps in her chair. Mr Phillips is stunned for a moment then moves to the shattered window. Laughing voices are heard and someone shouts, 'Go to work on a brick.' Mr Phillips returns to console Mrs Phillips who sits bolt upright, trembling and crying.)

MR PHILLIPS Come and lay down, dear, then I'll go next door and phone the police again.

MRS PHILLIPS You know you're wasting your time. *(Door bell rings.)*

MR PHILLIPS *(picking up a walking stick)* If it's those kids from that Comprehensive again, I'll show them what for.

(Mr Phillips disappears and returns with the social worker, who is speaking.)

SOCIAL WORKER Have you had the letter yet about your free holiday? *(Seeing the weeping old woman)* Why, Mrs Phillips, what's the matter? *(Then, seeing the damage everywhere)* What's happened? Who did it? Not the kids from the Comprehensive School again!

MR PHILLIPS Yes, the new glass had only been in the window two days. That's it, we can't go.

SOCIAL WORKER What do you mean – you can't go?

MR PHILLIPS We can't go away on holiday and leave our home to be smashed into again and again by those thugs. It's the parents' fault. The police say that the head-teacher can't trace who's doing it.

MRS PHILLIPS *(now calmed)* That's the second time in a week. We can't go on holiday and leave our home to that.

SOCIAL WORKER We could board up the window. You must take this free holiday. You both need the break, all this stress will make you ill.

MR PHILLIPS   No, that's final. We cannot go and leave our home. I fought for this country in the last war and all my friends were killed. We never thought we were saving this country to become fit only for young thugs. I ran a youth club in the '50s and the youngsters were polite and nice then. Whatever has happened to them?

COMMENT   This is a true story. If we could interview the three pupils who did such a cowardly and sickening thing they would tell us they did it for 'kicks', 'for a laugh'. They'd say that old people are 'finished' anyway. Remember these facts:

READER A   Fact number one – your grandparents are old people.

READER B   Fact number two – your parents will, in a few years' time, be old people.

READER C   Fact number three – you will one day be an old person.

READER D   Fact number four – we are all equal in God's sight, whatever our age; and each one of us will die.

COMMENT   Christ did not tell us to love the people we like or those of our own age group. He said:

READER A   Love one another as I have loved you. *John 15:12*

READER B   What I command you is to love one another. *John 15:17*

READER C   Whatsoever you do to the least person you do to me. *Matthew 25:40*

HYMN   *A new commandment.* HON 1, HONS 39, HONA 4
Whatsoever you do. HON 452, HONS 606

F52 Street children

OPENING RECORD *Money, money, money,* Abba. Abba's Greatest Hits. Epic. *(Fade after 30 seconds.)*

COMMENT Money is important in life, but what if you are a young person, and
- you have no money
- you have no home
- you have no family
- you have no adults helping you. What then?

You are a street child. A young person living on the streets of a big city. Every poor country in the Southern Hemisphere (Third World) has big cities and street children.

READER A Father Patrick Shanahan works among the street children of Africa, in the city of Accra, the capital of Ghana. There are about 11,000 children living on the streets of Accra, ranging in age from 5 to 17. These children live, work and sleep on the streets. There are also 3,000 street babies in Accra. These are babies born to young girls on the streets. Here are two true stories of street children whom Father Pat knows.

READER B Kwame is a 14-year-old shoe-shine boy. He sleeps each night at the lorry park of Accra, under one of the lorries for shelter. He wakes as soon as it gets light and buys some water from the local water lorry to wash with. By 6.30am Kwame will be looking for the women who sell food on the streets. If he has kept enough money from the day before he will buy some rice water or porridge, and a piece of bread. Then he will join the crowds heading for the city centre with his precious box of shoe-shining materials under his arm. He has his own patch of pavement but may have to fight another boy to drive him off, to protect his area.

Kwame will be there all day, through the terrible humid heat of the day. If he has a good day he may earn the equivalent of £1; if he has a bad day he will be hungry. Like most poor people Kwame spends 70% of what he earns on food and water. He finishes as it gets dark and heads back to the lorry park. Chances are that he will be fast asleep by 10 o'clock, having first paid for water to wash and to use a toilet. He will also pay a watchman to guard his shoe-shine box while he is asleep under a lorry. (Some street boys earn money by staying awake all night guarding the shoe-shine boys' boxes.)

READER C Ama is a small, chunky, pretty street girl of 13. She sleeps on a piece of land beside the central railway station in Accra. During the day it is an open market place, but here, on a normal night you can count at least 400 girls sleeping under the empty market stalls. During the day, when it is too hot for the market traders to move around the streets with their goods, Ama earns a few small coins as a load carrier.

Ama comes out from under the stalls at 6am; she usually doesn't wash because she earns so little she cannot afford the water. Sometimes she also goes hungry unless she can borrow some money from a friend. Ama starts looking for work as the stall-holders arrive. At present she can carry loads of about 25 kilos on her head, but as she grows older she will be able to earn more by carrying heavier loads. Ama has already been on the streets for three years and she is in constant danger of becoming pregnant. If she does, she will have to care for the baby on the streets and will find it even harder to find work and survive.

COMMENT   What would Jesus have to say about the lives of street children? When an event is recorded in all three of the Gospels, Matthew, Mark and Luke, you know that it must be important. Each of them tells how Jesus called children to him and blessed them.

SCRIPTURE READING   Matthew 19:13-15, or Mark 10:13-16, or Luke 18:15-17.

PRAYER   Almighty God, Father of us all,
we cannot begin to understand
how terrible it must be to have to live in such poverty
as that which is endured by the street children,
without homes or families;
with no health care or education.
May we appreciate how blessed we are
to have secure, comfortable lives.
May we remember to help the poor
whenever we have an opportunity
and to pray for them regularly. Amen.

HYMN   *God's Spirit is in my heart.* HON 152, HONS 183, HONA 180

F53 Option for the poor

ASSEMBLY LEADER *When all are settled, the leader numbers off, one to five, as many of those assembled as is practical. It may be the whole group (if it is small) or just the first two or three rows (if it is a large group). Then the leader asks number one in each five to stand up.*

(See F50 for an alternative way of opening this assembly.)

COMMENT If all the people in the world were represented by five people, those like us, who have comfortable lives, are represented by the one. We all know and need to take in that there are hundreds of millions of poor people in the world. Most of the people God loves are poor. It is clear from the Bible that God is very especially on the side of the poor.

READER A God spoke to the Jewish people through the words of the prophet Amos. 'You trample on the poor . . . therefore, though you have built stone mansions, you will not live in them.' *Amos 5:11*

READER B Amos the prophet warns the rich and comfortable people against depriving the poor of justice in the courts: 'seek good, not evil, so that you may live'. *Amos 5:14*

READER C At the very moment when Mary rejoices that she is truly the mother of the Messiah, the Son of God, she tells how God favours those who are in need. 'He has filled the hungry with good things, but has sent the rich away empty.' *Luke 1:53*

READER D Jesus himself was a poor person. He once said: 'Foxes have holes and birds of the air have nests, but the Son of Man has nowhere to lay his head.' *Matthew 8:20*

COMMENT Time after time, in the Bible, we find God making a positive declaration in favour of the poor. Jesus spoke up for the poor, the widows, the orphans, as did the prophets, particularly Isaiah, Amos and Micah. It is the obligation of the Church today to defend their interests. Let's hear what Cardinal Basil Hume, representing the Church, says:

READER Whenever the poor are afflicted or neglected, or whenever human freedom and dignity are not respected, then the Church has a duty to sound a prophet's note, and it must be prepared to be unpopular on matters which concern politicians as well.
Cardinal George Basil Hume OSB

COMMENT What then should we do? What does God require of us? The prophet Micah tells us:
'And what does the Lord require of you?
To act justly and to love mercy
and to walk humbly with your God.'
Micah 6:8

HYMN *There is a world.* HON 414, HONS 542
Christ's is the world. HONA 83

GENERAL THEMES

G54 Thanksgiving

OPENING RECORD *Thank you for the music, Abba. Abba's Greatest Hits, volume 2. (Fade after 1 minute 15 seconds.)*

READING The legend goes that two angels were once sent down from heaven, each with a basket. They went from place to place, to poor houses and rich houses visiting the children saying their prayers, and to the people in the churches, both young and old. Then at length they came flying back with their loads. The basket carried by one angel was full and heavy, but the other was almost empty and light – hardly worthwhile, one would have thought, to go so far and collect so little.

'What have you got in your basket?' asked one angel of the other.

'I was sent to collect the prayers of all the people who said to God, "I want" and "Please give me",' answered the angel who carried the heavy load. 'And what have you got in your basket?'

'Oh,' replied the other angel, sadly, 'I have been sent to collect the "thank yous" of all the people to whom our great God has sent a blessing, but see how few have remembered to give.'

COMMENT You may be wondering what the connection is between our opening recording, *Thank you for the music,* and the legend of the angels. The answer is that we take music for granted, just as we take for granted all God's other wonderful gifts.

RECORD *(As background to the following: Thank you for the music, Abba.)*

READER A Almighty God, we want to thank you for our lives and everything that makes them happy.

READER B Thank you for the TV and our favourite programmes – may we use TV well.

READER C Thank you for pop music and for all our favourite performers and musicians. May we learn to make music of our own, to give happiness to others.

READER D Thank you for Radio One (or local station) – may we never use it to annoy other people who do not share our tastes.

READER E Thank you for the game of football that gives pleasure to so many people. And especially thank you for helping our favourite teams to do well – may we always respect other people both when we watch and play football.

READER F Thank you for our homes, families, school, teachers and friends – may we always show love and respect to those around us.

COMMENT We are as we are. We cannot change our height, our looks, our gifts and talents, our brothers and sisters – or our parents or teachers. Accepting ourselves as we are, with all that we have or do not have, and being grateful for it, is an important key to happiness.

PRAYER Thank you, God, for filling things:
filling the world with people;
filling words with meaning;
filling life with happenings;
filling our plates with food and our purses with money.

May we ask for one thing?
Please fill our hearts with thankfulness.
May our gratitude overflow
in kindness and thoughtfulness towards everyone. Amen.

HYMN *Tell out, my soul.* HON 388, HONS 514, HONA 467
Now thank we all our God. HON 284, HONS 375, HONA 354

G55 Freedom

COMMENT The *Daily Mail* of 20 December 1997 carried the banner headline 'THE GIRL IN A CAGE', with the photograph of a 4-year-old little girl sitting and crying inside a wooden cage. Here is the story:

READING 1 The torment is etched on her face as she stares out from the tiny cage that has been her home for two years. Even if she were a dog, the treatment meted out to Lourdes Gomez would be considered barbaric. When she was 2, Lourdes was locked in the bamboo prison by her parents simply for being 'a nuisance'. There she stayed – suspended over a pigsty – until a visitor to her parents' house spotted her shivering in the cold and alerted police in Mexico's central state of San Luis Potosi.

COMMENT The young girl was released and her parents went to prison for taking away her freedom.
Freedom is a wonderful human right that even God respects.

READING 2 The whole story of how God chose to become a human being is totally amazing. The infinite, all-powerful, all-knowing Spirit, who holds in existence the immeasurable universe of a billion galaxies (galaxies, notice, not just stars!), galaxies that are 400 million light years apart, asked a 13-year-old Jewish peasant girl if she would consider being the human mother of the Godhead! And God waited for a reply.
Mary had been assured, at the beginning of the request, that she need not worry; 'Do not be afraid', the messenger said. Then, after a down-to-earth question about how it was going to be possible, since she was a virgin, Mary said, 'Let what you have said be done to me'; in other words, God received the 'yes' he was waiting and hoping for! The infinite Creator respects human freedom.
Tony Castle, 'Love Comes'

COMMENT God respects our freedom; do we respect one another's freedom?
Do we really understand that freedom brings responsibilities?

VOICE A Freedom for me means staying out as long as I like at night.

VOICE B Freedom for me means doing what I like – at home and at school.

VOICE C Freedom for me means wearing what I like, when I like and how I like.

VOICE D Freedom for me means no rules and regulations – no police, no teachers telling you what to do.

COMMENT But is that real freedom? Listen carefully to what some famous and wise people have said about real freedom.

READER A Gandhi said, 'Freedom is not worth having if it does not include the freedom to make mistakes.'

READER B   Field-Marshal Lord Montgomery said, 'True freedom is freedom to do what we ought to do. It is not freedom to do as we like.'

COMMENT   So real freedom does not keep saying 'I want', 'I must have'. Freedom does not come from disrespecting others – from pushing yourself forward with no concern for other people's rights and freedoms, especially the needy and the weak.

READER C   Christ came to make all humans free.
Free from their isolation and their fear.
He came –
>   homeless – and so at home among all;
>   in poverty – and so the guest of all;
>   in weakness – and so at the mercy of all;
>   common – and so approachable by all;
a man with time for all,
a man for others.
Jim Bates

PRAYER   Almighty Father,
you made us to be free.
Help us, who want to be free,
to understand what true freedom is
so that we will not be caught
in the tyranny of our own self-love.
May we learn to imitate the most free of all men,
Jesus Christ, who gave himself for others.
We ask this through the same Christ our Lord. Amen.

HYMN   *Peace is flowing like a river.* HON 341, HONS 442, HONA 412

G56 Hope

OPENING RECORD   *Chiquitita,* Abba. Abba's Greatest Hits. Epic.

COMMENT   The song says, 'Sing a new song – the sun is still shining above you'. That is what hope is; continuing to believe that even on the gloomiest winter day we know that high above the clouds the sun is there, ready to break through.

READING   News headline.   Rachel – the girl saved by love.
                                 Doctors gave up hope, but her family battled on!

When doctors gave up hope for coma girl, Rachel Neal, her devoted family brought her home from hospital – and saved her with love. As the eleven-year-old lay unconscious after a serious road accident, her grip on life was so frail that medical staff spoke of using her organs for transplants when the end came. They gave up hope and turned off the ventilator. Her family were allowed to take her home to die.

But back in her own bedroom, her mother, Doreen, sat beside her and prayed; she begged Rachel to give her some hope. After six weeks in a deep coma, Rachel answered her mother's prayers . . . with a tiny flicker of her eyelids. 'I told her I had to have a sign that she could hear me and asked her to blink,' Mrs Neal recalled. 'She did . . . at first I thought maybe I was hoping too much for a miracle. But I asked her to blink three times, then four, then five. She did!'

Six months after the road accident that nearly claimed her life, Rachel is back, fully recovered.

COMMENT   That wonderful story from a daily newspaper is a perfect illustration of the old proverb: 'While there's life, there's hope.'

No matter how bad we feel things are, we should always hope and, of course, pray.

READING   To hope means to be ready
at every moment
for that which is not yet born,
and yet not become desperate
if there is no birth in our lifetime.
There is no sense in hoping
for that which already exists
or for that which cannot be.
Those whose hope is weak
settle down for comfort or for violence;
those whose hope is strong
see and cherish all signs of new life
and are ready every moment
to help the birth
of that which is ready to be born.
Erich Fromm

PRAYER   Lord,
it's just when we most need
the light of your love in our lives
that we least feel like asking for it.

When things go wrong
and life seems dismal and grey
and hardly worth living,
be with us, Lord, to support and strengthen us.
Help us never to forget
that your Son, the light of the world,
is always smiling upon us;
ready to lift us up
and fill our lives again with hope.
Please hear our prayer through the same Christ our Lord. Amen.

HYMN   *Lord of all hopefulness.* HON 250, HONS 329, HONA 313
God is love. HON 148, HONS 178, HONA 169

G57 Stewardship of our planet

COMMENT Do you know the old saying,
'Red sky at night, shepherd's delight;
red sky in the morning, shepherd's warning'?
That's a very old weather saying. Even the Jews of the time of Jesus had a similar version of it.

READING The Pharisees and the Sadducees came, and to test him they asked if he would show them a sign from heaven. He replied, 'In the evening you say, "It will be fine; there is a red sky," and in the morning, "Stormy weather today; the sky is red and overcast." You know how to read the face of the sky, but you cannot read the signs of the times.' *Matthew 16:1-3*

COMMENT What are the signs of our times?

READING *Yoruba poem from West Africa*

Enjoy the earth gently.
Enjoy the earth gently
for if the earth is spoiled
it cannot be repaired.
Enjoy the earth gently.

READING We in the Third World are destroying our environment. We are forced to cut down the wood to make fuel so that we can cook. We cut down the wood to sell to the cities, to make a living. In fifteen years there will be no trees left in Ghana. I tell you: there is only one way to solve the threat to the environment. Poverty must be eliminated. How? You must have less. We must have more. You must sacrifice to give. You must give out of love. *Bernard Guri, Ghanaian agriculturist*

READING A man was walking along a road when he saw a woman planting a tree. The man asked her, 'How many years will it take for this tree to bear fruit?' The woman answered that it would take seventy years.

The man asked, 'Are you so fit and strong that you expect to live that long and eat its fruit?'

The woman answered, 'I found a fruitful world because my ancestors planted for me. So I will do the same for my children.' *Anon*

SCRIPTURE READING We are members of God's family, and I ask you to remember two things: keep God's kindness always in your minds, and give yourselves heart and soul to him – your energy, your heart and your mind. You belong to God, and it is service like this that makes God glad. Don't try to do 'what everybody else does'; let God keep your mind alive and ready to think new thoughts, and you'll be a very different person from what you were. In this way you will be able to find out what God wants you to be and to do – what is worth while and right and grown-up. *Romans 12:1-5 (New World)*

COMMENT 'Think new thoughts.' We must have the courage to think about the future; what will our children find? If we do not look after our planet now, what will there be left for future generations? 'Don't try to do "what everybody else does".' As Christians we must care for and take responsibility for the beautiful world placed into our care by God.

PRAYER Lord God,
we thank you for the beauty and fruitfulness
of the world you have given to us.
Please forgive us for taking it for granted,
and help us to take seriously our responsibility
to care for all your creation as you care for us.
We ask this through Jesus Christ our Lord. Amen.

HYMN *All the nations of the earth.* HON 22, HONA 20, CHB 14
Fill your hearts with joy and gladness. HON 120, HONS 142, HONA 130

G58 Peace

ROLE-PLAY *Persons required for roles of mother, father, child and three voices. The family are sitting watching TV (side view of a cardboard box will do).*

VOICE 1 *(TV SET)* The news tonight is of renewed threats from Turkey against the Greek community of Cyprus. Airborne troops are on stand-by; the Greek Government has threatened to respond with nuclear weapons.

MOTHER Turn it over, dear, we don't want to hear that dismal news of people suffering – war, war, war. *(Child gets up and switches programme over.)*

VOICE 2 This evening's BBC 2 *Panorama* programme is on the parades issue in Northern Ireland. Violent conflict between Loyalists and Nationalists continues to be a problem . . .

FATHER Turn the telly over. See what's on ITV. *(Child, using the hand control, changes channels.)*

VOICE 3 *(PRECEDED BY A HAMMERING NOISE)* It is a great tragedy when a young mother has to barricade herself in her own home against a violent drunken husband. In our stressful society wife-battering seems to be on the increase . . . *(without a word the child gets up and turns the TV off).*

CHILD Why is life so violent, Dad? Is there no peace anywhere?

FATHER Well, at least there's peace in our home, isn't there!

COMMENT 'Why is life so violent?' What a difficult question! At least the father was right in pointing out that peace has always got to begin with us. Whether it is violence on the grand scale – war; or the smaller, but just as terrifying, scale of terrorist activities in our own country – or violence in a family: peace must begin with us.

POSTER *Made or at least written on a large sheet for the occasion, the words, 'Peace starts with a smile'.*

COMMENT *(As the poster is shown)* These are the words of the famous Mother Teresa, who says that peace must start with us. But a genuine smile means that you have peace inside yourself.

READING Peace is not won
by man's eternal strife.
Peace is the power of God
in human life.
It dwells with joy and love,
is manifest in grace;
the star above his crib,
the light that is his face. *Anon*

SONG WITH PRAYER   *Sing (or read) the following chorus between topical intercessions for peace.*

> Let there be peace shared among us
> let there be peace in our eyes.
> May now your peace sweep this nation,
> cause us, O Lord, to arise.
> Give us a fresh understanding
> filled with your peace that is real.
> Let there be peace shared among us,
> let there be peace.
> *From song 'Let there be love' by Dave Bilbrough*

READER   Let us pray for a true and lasting peace in Northern Ireland between all the different interests and communities.
Let there be peace shared among us . . .

READER   Let us pray for . . .
Let there be peace shared among us . . .

HYMN   *(If the above is read rather than sung.)*
Make me a channel of your peace. HON 262, HONS 342, HONA 328

G59 Aliens and unsolved mysteries

COMMENT Nowadays the scary stories on TV and in books are often about aliens; in former times it was ghost stories that scared people. Do you believe in ghosts? Poltergeists? UFOs?

Here is the first of two reported sightings in newspapers.

READING 1 At Broadhaven School, 14 children aged between 10 and 11 told their headmaster they had seen a UFO land 200 yards from where they were playing. He separated them and told them to draw what they saw. Their drawings matched. So did their reports. Headmaster Richard Llewelin said: 'Children of that age aren't capable of maintaining such an elaborate hoax.' It is an area bristling with defence establishments, some highly secret. The RAF confirmed a flood of reports, and said the sightings did not match their operations. *The Sun*

COMMENT Each year there are thousands of sightings of strange shapes up above us. Around 2,000 people, throughout the world, have claimed actually to have met UFO crews – humanoids. Is it all deception? A hoax? Do other intelligent beings visit our planet? Gordon Cooper, US astronaut, says this:

READING 2 'The American Space Agency and government know that intelligent beings from other planets visit our world. They have an enormous amount of evidence but have kept quiet.'

COMMENT UFOs are only part of the mysterious unseen world about us. What do you make of this report which appeared in the *Daily Mail*?

READING 3 On the evening of 6 August 1979, Madame Bourdat, of the little French village of Seron, was herding her few cows past an abandoned farmhouse when she noticed smoke billowing out of a downstairs room. She rushed to her neighbours, the Lahore family, who own the disused building and together they put the fire out.

Within two hours, two more mysterious fires broke out, this time in the Lahores' modern farmhouse. In the following few weeks 90 fires broke out; no one, yet, has succeeded in finding an explanation. Despite the efforts of mediums, psychologists, priests, exorcists and police and fire experts from Tarbes and Paris, no explanation or cause has yet come to light. Several witnesses have seen the fires begin. First there is a smell of smoke, then a charred spot appears which after a few moments bursts into flame. The burning object is rushed out of the house to be doused by one of the policemen on duty there. On one hair-raising day alone, 32 separate fires broke out in the house. At one time or another nearly every conceivable item in the house has been burned, even clothes while the Lahores were wearing them. No one on the spot, either in the Lahore family itself or from the constant stream of specialists and experts that have streamed through the house, has come up with an explanation. Police in Tarbes and Paris have had to admit that they can offer no help or guidance as to the cause of the strange happenings at the Lahore farmhouse.

COMMENT That story seems to point to poltergeists, but who knows? Of course, to believe in God is to believe in a spirit world, an unseen world. Many experts are seeking ways of exploring this unseen world in much the same way as the old explorers courageously discovered that the world was not flat, as was believed at the time. Whatever the explanation of these mysteries one thing is certain, God is still creator of all and master of all. Let us have a healthy interest and open and enquiring minds, but we must take care not to fill our minds with sensational rubbish.

SCRIPTURE READING Fill our minds with everything that is true, everything that is noble, everything that is good and pure, everything that we love and honour, and everything that can be thought virtuous or worthy of praise.
Philippians 4:8

COMMENT Our faith and trust at all times must be in Christ who is over all things.

SCRIPTURE READING He is the image of the unseen God and the first-born of all creation, for in him were created all things in heaven and on earth: everything visible and everything invisible, Thrones, Dominations, Sovereignties, Powers – all things were created through him and for him. Before anything was created, he existed, and he holds all things in unity. *Colossians 1:15-17*

HYMN *O Lord, my God.* HON 311, HONS 404, HONA 380
Immortal, invisible. HON 196, HONS 242, HONA 242

G60 Fashion

COMMENT   The latest fashions are very important to some people.

VOICE 1   I wear only Nike – Nike trainers, Nike sweat shirts, Nike is really cool.

VOICE 2   I wear Reebok trainers, jumpers – wouldn't wear anything else. Reebok's the really cool label.

VOICE 3   No, it's Kappa for me.

VOICE 4   You're joking – it's Adidas. They've got everything, not just trainers and stuff.

VOICE 5   You've no class – the really cool labels are Calvin Klein or Yves Saint Laurent.

COMMENT   The voices of the rich! Only in comfortable rich countries or among the very rich in Southern countries could such voices be heard.

Does what we wear tell people something about us? If we compete with one another over designer labels then we know that we live in a rich country. Do clothes tell us any more about a person? Do we sometimes judge people falsely because of what they are wearing?

READER   A young Catholic priest who works in Central London had two experiences on the same day that made him stop and think.

He was in the local Catholic Comprehensive school talking to a Year 9 class of students about what it was like to be a priest. A boy made a rude remark about wearing a white clerical collar and a black suit, and said, 'Does anyone treat you normally, dressed like that?'

In the afternoon the young priest visited a centre for the homeless and a distressed mother with two young children commented, 'It's all right for you, you go round in a posh black suit and everyone respects you because of who you are.'

After thinking about what had been said, the priest arranged to have a complete week off from his parish work. He went to a charity shop and bought the worst set of male clothes that he could find; sloppy, old and grubby. He told no one where he was going.

The next day, unshaved and unwashed, and wearing the old clothes, he slipped out of his house at 6 am and caught a red London bus to an area in South London known as the Elephant and Castle. He wandered along the street and sat on the ground in a doorway. He put out an old hat on the pavement and started begging. He sat there for a couple of hours until a policeman moved him on.

The young priest slept rough that night and discovered how cold it was. He was bullied by two younger homeless men who told him he was on their patch. He wandered and lived rough all the week.

On Sunday morning he went into Westminster Cathedral to the midday Mass. Several people got up and moved away from his row of seats when he sat down. At the sign of Peace no one was near and no one would shake his hand. As he left he overheard two elderly ladies complaining to the doorman that 'such people should not be allowed into church'.

His week ended and he returned to his parish a much wiser man. After he had celebrated an early Mass in his own church, he rushed across to get to the midday Mass at Westminster Cathedral. He went to the same place and the same people were in the pews. No one recognised the young priest in the smart black suit. However, everyone smiled and nodded to him; and when the sign of peace came every churchgoer close to him was eager to shake his hand.

At the end of the Mass the young priest asked those around him if he could have a few words with them. Drawing them aside he said, 'Do you remember the homeless man here at Mass last Sunday?'

'Yes,' one woman replied, 'it was disgusting. Such people should know their place and stay away from decent people.'

'I was that man,' the young priest said, 'and I am really disturbed that you call yourselves Christians and then judge people by what they wear.' He quietly left the uncomprehending group, and the cathedral.

COMMENT   We cannot imagine Jesus making such a judgement, can we? What did Jesus have to say about clothes and fashion?

READER   I tell you, do not worry about your life, what you will eat; or about your body, what you will wear. Life is more than food and the body more than clothes . . . (continue). *Luke 12:22-30*

COMMENT   Notice that Jesus says, 'Do not set your heart' on these things. So it is all right to be interested in fashion, but do not make it the most important thing in your life. And most of all do not judge anyone who dresses differently, or has no interest in clothes or fashion. You are not a better person because you wear Nike than someone else who can only afford cheaper clothes.

HYMN   *Do not worry over what to eat.* HONS 123, OS 60
Seek ye first. HON 362, HONS 473, HONA 442